Life
at the Top

D1403103

Life
at the Top

Tales, Truths, and
Trusted Recipes from the Mount
Washington Observatory

Eric Pinder

DOWN EAST BOOKS

Copyright © 1997 by Eric Pinder
Portions of this text have appeared in different form in *Appalachian Trailway News*.
ISBN 0-89272-396-3
Book design by Tim Seymour.
Front cover aerial photograph by Charles Feil.
Inga photograph by Al Oxton.
Color Separation by Roxmont Graphics.
Printed and bound at Bookcrafters, Inc.

5 4 3 2 1

Down East Books / Camden, Maine

LIBRARY OF CONGRESS CATALOGING-IN-PUBLICATION DATA

Pinder, Eric, 1970–
    Life at the top : tales, truths, and trusted recipes from the Mount Washington
    Observatory / Eric Pinder.
        p.   cm.
    Includes index.
    ISBN 0-89272-396-3 (pbk.)
    1. Mount Washington Observatory—Employees—Social conditions. 2.
Washington, Mount (N.H.)—Climate. I. Title.
QC875.U72M6855   1997
551.69742'1—dc21
                                                            97-11519
                                                            CIP

For Lynne

Acknowledgments

The Observatory's summit crew deserves a tremendous thank-you for helping to make this book a reality. Special thanks are due to Mark Ross-Parent, Lynne Host, Steve Piotrow (despite his frustrating habit of beating me at Scrabble), Norm Michaels, and Mike Courtemanche.

I also want to extend many thanks to Jennifer Morin, for reading and commenting on earlier drafts of this book; Peter Crane, for his inexhaustible reservoir of wisdom, patience, and bad jokes; and Guy Gosselin, for advice and support in starting this project.

Thanks also to my editor, Karin Womer, for her skillful surgery with the blue pencil. I'm grateful to Sarah Shor, Tim Ewald, and Barbara Shor for many years of friendship and encouragement. Special thanks are also due to Susan Ross-Parent and Meredith Piotrow, who have fed a starving writer on more than one occasion.

Former Observers Greg Gordon and Al Oxton deserve credit for many of the spectacular photographs preserved (anonymously) in the Observatory archives.

I also want to thank the many staff members, Observatory volunteers and friends who contributed recipes or suggestions to this book: Eric Kaatz, Dave Thurlow, Chris Uggerholt, Jacob "Jetstream" Klee, Mary Simpson, Kathy Bojack, Sara Curtis, Ira Seskin, Helen Gerard, Norma "Sunshine" King, Jane Pinder (*a k a* "Mom"), park ranger Danny Johnson, Jude Chauvette, Ken Rancourt, Terry Ferrara, Sharon Jeffrey, Mike Colcough, Jill Schoof, Pete Lespasio (for salad-making prowess that is now legendary), Doug Thompson, and Bonnie Logan. Your help and enthusiasm are what made this book happen.

Contents

Introduction:
An Iceberg in the Sky

Who would have guessed that the windiest, most wintry weather in the world occurs not in the Himalayas or on the icy tundra of Antarctica, but right here in the hills and mountains of New England?

On Mount Washington, highest peak in the Presidential Range of New Hampshire, blizzards regularly pummel the summit, sometimes even in summer. Bone-numbing cold, frequent fog, and furious winds have earned this lofty mountain a nickname: "Home of the World's Worst Weather."

This is a book about Mount Washington and its savage skies and the unusual lives of the handful of people who eat, sleep, work, and play in a land above the clouds.

Mount Washington is a 400-million-year-old spike of metamorphic rock thrusting high above the hills of New Hampshire. Expansive views of sparkling blue lakes and rolling hills entice thousands of sightseers to climb up the slopes to its 6,288-foot summit each summer. They visit when the temperature and wind are relatively mild: gentle breezes caress the brows of weary hikers like a cool, damp cloth. But in winter the weather turns formidable—sometimes deadly. Whenever I strap on my winter hiking boots and scramble up a high ridge on the mountain, I brace against the nearly constant wind. Gusts scissor through my jacket and hurl chunks of ice the size of cinder blocks into the sky. My nose reddens, and I fight back a sneeze. A powerful gust knocks me sideways, like a punch delivered by a strong invisible hand.

At any time of year, the mountain may be swept by winds so strong they can hoist me into the sky like a kite. Rather than walk, I must fly down the trail; the flaps of my jacket flutter against my ribs like wings. I wobble to keep my balance and try to walk in a straight line. All across the summit cone, I see other hikers buffeted by wind. They walk in jerky, mechanical steps through the gusts, like marionettes with missing strings.

Despite these extreme conditions—or, more accurately, because of them—Mount Washington is home to a small crew of scientists who live and work on the windy summit, keeping track of the notorious weather.

The Mount Washington Observatory was established as a private non-profit organization in 1932 to study weather and climate trends. The Observatory's wintry conditions attract scientists and other researchers who are studying cold-weather climates. "We're really an arctic island in a temperate zone," explains staff meteorologist Mark Ross-Parent. "There's something about weather extremes that people love."

A healthy sense of humor helps the staff to take demanding conditions in stride. Mark boasts that he has "the highest paying job in New England." Unfortunately, that refers to his elevation, not his wages. "Working here really limits your upward mobility," another meteorologist quips. A former employee, back on the summit for a visit, also chimes in: "As soon as I left this job, my career went downhill."

Two crews work on the summit on alternate weeks, and their duties include scientific research, weather reporting, daily radio broadcasts—and, of course, shoveling snow: "Wow! Two days in a row of strange white stuff. I think it could be snow, but there's so darn much of it, I can't really be sure," writes one scientist in the Observatory logbook on a January day. A little later he adds: "The sledding should be fairly decent tomorrow. The crew (all two of us) spent the day shoveling, but it seems to be blowing right back in, so that all evidence of our hard work will be gone by tomorrow. Memo to the other shift: We really did shovel. Really! Trust us."

Life at the Top takes a look at life on the summit, where workdays are punctuated by visits from wild foxes and soaring ravens. In daylight, we catch glimpses of flying-saucer-shaped lenticular clouds in orbit around the peaks. Clear nights sometimes bring spectacular views of meteor showers or the aurora borealis. Swirling snow wraps around us like a blindfold in winter, forcing us to retreat indoors. And at dinner time, the aroma of a spicy spinach quiche wafts up from the kitchen.

Quiche? Would you believe that people who are crazy enough to sled down the six-thousand-foot-high mountain in the raw grip of January can also be gourmet cooks? Workers on Mount Washington endure the worst blows of winter weather, but they compensate by eating well—and often—so any book about the Observatory crew's trials and triumphs naturally must include a selection of favorite recipes. You'll find them beginning on page 67.

"If you don't like the weather, wait a minute," is an old Yankee aphorism. On Mount Washington, they say it with a twist: "If you don't like the weather, go someplace else!" But have a bite to eat before you go.

LYNNE HOST

Rime ice can form on exposed surfaces even in early summer.

The Story in the Stones—
Mount Washington's Geology

For obvious reasons, Mount Washington is called "The Rockpile" by the hardy souls who live and work on its windy summit. Jagged boulders jut through the clouds, and stones tumble down the trails, kicked loose by hikers' boots. Steep ravines and rocky ridges cut across the skyline, thousands of feet above timberline. But where did this jumble of stones come from? To read the clues in the rocks themselves, we must climb to the summit, close our eyes, and strain to imagine the events of the distant past. Only in our minds can we witness the tumultuous evolution of Mount Washington.

GLACIERS

According to the best scientific lore, at the height of the last ice age, a glacier scraped across the mountain, scattering stones and boulders from distant lands (glacial erratics) on the slopes. ("But where is the glacier now?" a curious visitor to the summit once asked a north-country native. Replied that crusty old New England Yankee, "Ma'am, it's gone back for another load!") Although frost action accounts for most of the broken boulders we see above timberline, glacial ice has certainly left its signature on the summit. Mount Washington is like a work of art, a statue more than 400 million years in the making. Glaciers were the chisels that applied the final touches.

Where did the glaciers come from? At the start of the Pleistocene Era, roughly two million years ago, climatic instabilities produced worldwide fluctuations in temperature. Four ice ages, each lasting tens of thousands of years, occurred in the Pleistocene. During each one, vast sheets of ice spread across much of North America, burying New England's mountains, including Mount Washington.

Before the last ice age, Mount Washington was a taller and rounder mountain, much like those of the Great Smokies today. The Great Gulf, Tuckerman Ravine, and other steep, jagged cliffs that plunge down the mountainside are relatively new features, sculpted by glaciers.

At its peak, the ice sheet was more than a mile thick, a weight so heavy that the land beneath it sank. Every land mass on Earth "floats" on a layer of hot, liquid magma (molten lava deep underground), which gives it a special kind of buoyancy. If a cement block is placed on the deck of a tiny sailboat, the boat's hull sinks lower in the water. Similarly, a great weight like an ice cap—or a mountain range—tends to press down on the land around it. When the ice melts or the mountains erode, the burden becomes lighter and the landscape rebounds.

The New England landscape has risen and fallen many times during the past 500 million years. As recently as fifteen thousand years ago, the weight of a continental ice cap pressed down on the New England landscape like a firm hand. Later, when the glaciers melted and the weight disappeared, the land recoiled like an ancient rusty spring. Glacial erratics—rocks carried to the mountain from distant locations—are proof that an ice sheet once covered Mount Washington.

SCULPTED BY ICE

Many features shaped by glaciation are visible from the summit, the Mount Washington Auto Road, or the hiking trails.

Cirques are giant U-shaped valleys gouged out of the mountainside by valley glaciers. The last of these small glaciers melted away more than six thousand years ago, long after the continental ice sheet had retreated. Tuckerman Ravine and the Great Gulf are both cirques.

Tarns are basins scraped into the rocks by the motion of ice as glaciers slid across the land. These ice age potholes later filled with water, forming high-altitude ponds such as the Lakes of the Clouds. These lakes, huddled below the north slope of Mount Monroe, are the highest freshwater ponds in the Northeast. They are easily viewed from the flat rocks south of the TV building on the summit of Mount Washington.

Roches moutonées. As the great ice sheet spread across North America, it scooped up stones, gravel, and boulders and carried them south. Like a continent-sized piece of sandpaper, the glacier and its load of debris scraped across the mountains, sanding smooth the north slopes and "plucking off" the southern edges. Many rocky outcroppings in New England possess a long, gently sloping north side with a nearly vertical drop to the south. They are called sheepbacks, whalebacks, or *roches moutonées.* Mount Monroe is a giant sheepback, with a gentle slope in the northwest (the direction of the advancing glacier) and a jagged cliff in the southeast.

Glacial striations. A glance at many of the boulders above tree line reveals pale white lines running in a northwest-to-southeast direction. These are scars left behind by the continental ice sheet.

AFTER THE GLACIERS' RETREAT

When the Wisconsin Ice Age ended, approximately eight thousand years ago, the newly exposed landscape looked like a subarctic tundra. Ice had stripped away trees, grasses, and soil, and most animal species had fled south in search of warmer climates. Gradually, however, spruces, firs, and other trees returned, and with them came the animal species that continue to inhabit the woods of New England today.

As the climate warmed, hundreds of arctic plants and animals that had moved into New England during the last ice age could no longer survive— except on windy peaks above tree line, where the climate was still subarctic. Flowers such as *Diapensia lapponica* and Lapland rosebay are alpine refugees, stranded above tree line on Mount Washington and a few other high peaks in the Northeast.

METAMORPHIC ROCKS

Of course, ice is just a brief chapter in the long story of Mount Washington. Surprisingly, in our search for the origins of the highest peak in New England, we must first look far beneath the sea.

The stones that sit today on the summit of Mount Washington were born during the Paleozoic Era, some 400 million years ago, when layers of sand and mud were deposited in shallow seas and compressed into sedimentary rock in a swampy region near the Earth's equator. Over the course of many millions of years, these shallow waters disappeared as our continent drifted north into colder climates.

Three hundred million years ago, the continents of Europe and Africa rubbed against the coast of North America, squeezing out the ocean in between. As a result of this collision, miles of sedimentary rock were crumpled deep inside the Earth's mantle. Sandstones and shales that had long ago formed in New England's ancient seas were slowly metamorphosed by intense heat and pressure. Metamorphic rocks known as schist, gneiss, and quartzite were the result. Today, these rocks sit atop Mount Washington.

Why do the rocks sparkle? On rare days when the sun actually peeks through the clouds, boulders on Mount Washington's summit glitter and gleam. Each stone is studded with tiny mirrorlike plates of mica, a soft, easily scratched mineral that forms in paper-thin sheets. Mica is created when

How big is a million?

Geologists measure time in vast epochs of millions and billions of years. Lesser spans of time such as a month or a year—or even a century—are simply too small to use.

For example, the Paleozoic Era, in which the rocks of Mount Washington first formed, lasted 325 million years. That equals a whopping 3,900,000,000 months, or 118,706,250,000 days.

If we tried to count to a million (1,000,000) without pausing to eat or sleep, the task would take nearly two weeks. Counting to a billion (1,000,000,000) would require thirty-one years.

sedimentary rocks such as sandstone or shale are metamorphosed deep below the Earth's surface. The mineral is one clue that helps geologists unlock the mysteries of Mount Washington's past.

By looking at the texture and mineral content of rocks, geologists can determine the temperature and pressure at which these rocks formed. In the case of Mount Washington, sedimentary rocks made of clay, sand, and mud were at one time squeezed and heated several miles underground. The pressure at these depths was six kilobars, six thousand times stronger than the pressure on the Earth's surface. That's enough to instantly flatten a pickup truck into a tiny sliver of steel. The temperature in this geological pressure cooker was 1,100°F, a far cry from the annual average of 26.5°F that the rocks of the summit experience today.

Why are the rocks wavy or bent? High temperatures and pressures tend to make rock elastic. Just as metal bends and ruptures during a car crash, the bedrock was "crumpled" by the impact of Europe and Africa against the coast of North America roughly 300 million years ago.

Folded metamorphic rocks on Mount Washington.

Was Mount Washington once a volcano? New Hampshire is known as the Granite State, but granite is actually extremely rare on Mount Washington. Granite is a rock formed from magma. Geologists once believed that no granite (nor any other igneous or volcanic material) existed on Mount Washington. You can find granitic material on the slopes, just not very much. The primary bedrock in the Presidential Range is mica schist, a metamorphic rock. Mount Washington was never a volcano.

Are there any fossils on the mountain? No fossils have been discovered on Mount Washington, though fossils from the Mesozoic Era exist elsewhere in New England, particularly in the Connecticut River valley. The clay, sandstone, and mudstone that first formed the rocks of Mount Washington predate all but the earliest life on Earth. Whatever earlier fossils once existed in those ancient rocks were probably "cooked" away by intense heat and pressure when the original sedimentary rocks were metamorphosed into today's schist, quartzite, and gneiss. (Gneiss is pronounced "nice," which leads geologists to joke about "nice rocks." In earthquake-prone areas—near fault lines—some geologists have been known to stand amid the wreckage and quip, "It's not my fault!")

A Tour through Time

The Rockpile has passed through millions of years of heat and cold, rain and drought, upheaval and decay. Mount Washington's summit, currently the highest point of land in New England, long ago lay at the bottom of the sea. What geological events brought about this change? To get to the roots of Mount Washington's history, we must first delve deep into the past.

Our imaginary trip through time begins more than 500 million years ago, in the early Paleozoic Era. Mount Washington does not yet exist. In fact, no solid ground at all exists in the region that will one day be known as New Hampshire. Our time machine splashes down in a warm Paleozoic sea. Soon we must wade waist-deep through shallow waters. A tropical sun glares down at us, and tiny eyeless animals called trilobites scurry in the mud and sand at our feet.

Let's fast-forward through the next 10 million years. Layers of sand and mud thicken and harden into stone. (Far, far in the future, these rocks and others like them will rise from the sea to a height of 6,288 feet, forming the jagged tip of Mount Washington).

Another 10 million years spin by in the blink of an eye. Staring down into murky pools of water, we see the faces of trilobites sprout eyes. Distant continents lurch from the tropics and creep north, inch by inch. If we gaze at this faraway land through a telescope, we see nothing but stark, naked rock, unclothed by plants or trees. Not a single blade of grass waves in the wind.

Again, millions of years pass by. In time, the blue outlines of Europe and Africa appear on the horizon. The two continents swim closer year by year. The ocean starts to close.

Deep beneath the surface of the waves, the continental plates of North America, Europe, and Africa nudge together. A string of island volcanoes erupts and spews fire into the water.

The time is now 350 million years B.C.E. (Before the Common Era). The first primitive trees start to clothe the land; a stubble of needles and cones covers the rolling plains as new species of plant life spread a green swath across the continents. In the seas, the trilobites have long since gone extinct, and their fossils are empty shells, death masks embedded in the rocks.

Out on the ocean, volcanic islands slowly sink into the sea, a process that takes millions of years. The ocean continues to close. As the Old World starts to rub against the New, rocks made from hardened lava smash against the coastline of North America. During the impact, the sedimentary rocks we have been standing on are thrust deep underground, where they are squeezed and folded as the continents collide. In the depths of the Earth, heat and pressure melt the ancient sedimentary rocks at our feet, cooking a stew of mica and quartz. For an eon, these rocks and minerals—and our imaginary time capsule—are buried miles below the surface, boiling at a temperature of 1,110°F. But at long last, the mica-schist bedrock of Mount Washington is created.

Soon the proto-Atlantic Ocean is gone. In its place, the continents of Europe, Africa, and North America are firmly welded together into one supercontinent. We have arrived at the start of the Mesozoic Era, the Age of Reptiles, 245 million years ago.

The impact of the Old World against the coast of North America has thrust up a mountain range as high as today's Rockies. While we watch, the blur of a million seasons wears the mountains down.

Tiny reptiles dash and dart among the rocks, the earliest reptilian ancestors of dinosaurs. The time is 240 million years in the past. From a window in our time capsule, we see a crack appear between the Americas and the Old World. At long last, the Atlantic Ocean is born, a sliver of blue water splitting the world in two.

The early Appalachian mountains continue to erode for millions of years. Soil and minerals wash down streams into the newborn sea. As the mountains shrink in size, a great weight is lifted from the shoulders of the land; the ground rises. Somewhere far below the surface, a rock that will one day sit atop Mount Washington inches toward the surface.

During the next 200 million years, the shadow of Europe pulls away across a widening Atlantic Ocean. The tiny lizards evolve into dinosaurs and flourish. Little do they know that they will soon follow the trilobites into the oblivion of extinction.

The time is now 70 million years B.C.E. From the safety of our time capsule, we watch an asteroid streak through the atmosphere and explode off the coast of Mexico. Its impact rattles the Earth, spewing millions of tons of dust into the sky and blocking the warm rays of the sun. As plants wither and die, starving animals stagger across the land in search of food. During the chill years that follow, nearly 75 percent of all life on Earth vanishes—including the last of the dinosaurs.

When the dust finally clears, surviving species crawl out of the shadows. The Earth is reborn. Sixty-five million years ago, plants burst into flower for the first time, and hundreds of species of grasses roll across the plains, waving like banners in the wind.

But what about Mount Washington? After millions of years of erosion, millions of years lurking in the depths, the tip of New England's highest peak finally pokes through the surface. The mountain is later chipped and hewed by wind, rain, and ice, until at last it resembles the familiar cone-shaped mountain we know today. Much of the fine sculpture-work on Mount Washington occurred during the ice ages of the last two million years. If we travel in our time capsule to the start of the Pleistocene Epoch, we see that the mountain has risen from the depths and is now a high peak.

From the summit, we watch a tongue of ice ooze down from the northern tundra, flattening forests and scraping away the soil. Gradually, an

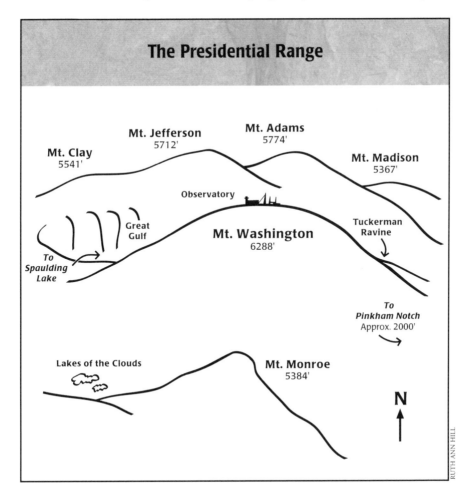

The Presidential Range

Mt. Clay
5541'

Mt. Jefferson
5712'

Mt. Adams
5774'

Mt. Madison
5367'

Observatory

Great
Gulf

Mt. Washington
6288'

Tuckerman
Ravine

To
Spaulding
Lake

To
Pinkham Notch
Approx. 2000'

Lakes of the Clouds

Mt. Monroe
5384'

N

RUTH ANN HILL

enormous ice sheet nudges against the base of Mount Washington. It sweeps around the mountain to the south, dipping its icy paws in the sea.

Thousands of years pass, and the ice layer thickens. Mount Jefferson and the rest of the northern Presidential Range soon succumb to the ice and disappear beneath it. Mount Washington appears as a snowy mound, protruding just a few hundred feet above the ice. Soon, it too is buried by the glacier.

The time is now 20,000 years in the past. The glacier scrapes across the mountain and carves a pair of basins in the rock. Later, these basins fill with water. Today, we call them Lakes of the Clouds.

Ten thousand years pass, and the climate warms. The continental ice sheet slowly melts away until the land we know as New England is free of ice, exposed to the sun. It is an ugly rubble heap of broken rock, stripped of soils and trees. On Mount Washington, small valley glaciers—chunks of ice as large as small hills—linger on the slopes. Gradually, these tiny glaciers pry open chasms called cirques in Tuckerman Ravine and the Great Gulf.

The time is now 6,000 years ago, and the valley glaciers have dwindled. Only a small hillock of snow snuggled in Tuckerman Ravine remains. For six thousand winters, right up to the present day, frost seeps into nooks and niches on Mount Washington. House-sized boulders split and crumble, pulled apart by fingers of ice. Streams of lichen-covered boulders cascade down the slopes, landing in piles of rubble in the basins. As soil and plants return to New England, a softwood forest creeps up the mountain's lower slopes.

Finally, after a journey that has lasted for 500 million years, our time capsule returns us to the Rockpile as it is today.

The World's Worst Weather— And What Causes It

You've probably heard the old expression, "March comes in like a lion and goes out like a lamb." How about, "A cold May is good for corn and hay"? Both of these tidbits of weather wisdom originated as folklore hundreds of years ago and were passed down from generation to generation.

Weather folklore played a crucial role in the lives of our ancestors. For farmers in New England, especially, failure to keep a close eye on the weather led to poor harvests and widespread famine. "Make hay while the sun shines," was a particularly popular piece of weather folklore. The only problem was, our ancestors had no way of knowing for certain whether the sun *would* shine. They couldn't rely on satellite images or watch a snappily dressed TV meteorologist give a forecast on the evening news. Instead, they looked to the only weather forecaster available: Mother Nature.

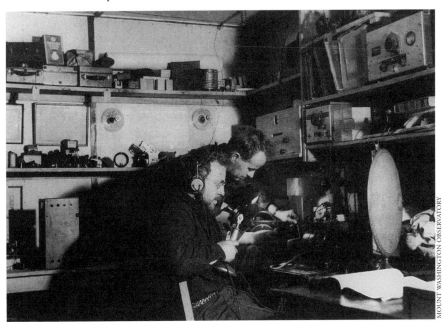

Joe Dodge and radioman Alex McKenzie in the original Observatory building during the winter of 1932–33.

The natural world is full of clues about weather. For example, consider the old saying, "As the days lengthen, so the cold strengthens." During the icy blue days of January and February, before spring rains washed away winter, people in New England huddled by their fires to keep warm, but they still had hope for the coming harvest season: "If February gives much snow, a fine summer it doth foreshow."

Unfortunately, weather has always been a fickle creature, and even the most popular folklore sayings sometimes get it wrong. Despite a wealth of

Forecasting the Weather

"If Mount Washington has the world's worst weather, doesn't that make you the world's worst weather forecasters?" jokes a wiseacre who's visiting the summit for the first time. As a reward for his quip, we make him wash the dishes.

The idea of a forecast for weather originated in the 1850s, when a British meteorologist named Fitzroy predicted the weather for the Board of Trade. Newspapers in England introduced weather forecasting to the public in 1861, but with no satellites and a poor understanding of the mechanics of weather, results were mixed at best. Still, a bad guess about the weather is better than no guess at all, so the new forecasts proved popular with the public. In fact, they were so popular that when the government shut them down in 1865, people demanded that the forecasts be brought back.

Weather forecasting started in earnest in the United States a few years later. For a while, daily forecasts were mailed to subscribers on postcards, a practice that ended in the 1920s when "free" forecasts over the radio came into play.

Today, with Doppler radar and computer models, the science of weather forecasting in the New England mountains has been taken to new heights (no pun intended). Despite advances in forecasting and meteorology, the weather can still catch us by surprise. Every so often, the sky clobbers us with a storm just to remind us that we still have a lot to learn.

weather wisdom, our ancestors were still caught by surprise by sudden storms and killing frosts. "Never trust a July sky," they vowed.

Even today, here in New England, we grudgingly acknowledge the fickle nature of weather. "If you don't like the weather here. . . ." You know the rest. Apparently, the only unchanging thing about weather is that it *always* changes.

WIND

Mount Washington's infamous weather reputation is mostly due to its winds. All year long, rivers of wind cascade across the cold stones and slither down the slopes. The wind refuses to stop, even when the air turns warm and the storms of winter wither in the sun. In fact, spring is the season when Mount Washington first entered the record books for wild

The old Observatory building, which was torn down and replaced by the Sherman Adams Summit Building in 1980.

weather. Mount Washington's reputation for fierce winds was firmly cemented on the stormy evening of April 12, 1934, when a gust howled across the summit at 231 miles per hour. No stronger wind has ever been measured on the Earth's surface.

History calls it "the Big Wind." In 1934, that record-breaking (and window-breaking) blast of icy air was closely monitored by meteorologists at the Mount Washington Observatory. In fact, the fury of the wind was less remarkable than the fact that humans witnessed the brunt of that storm and survived to tell the tale.

To instill confidence in the Observatory crew during savage storms— or at least to allay their fears of being scooped up and dashed against the rocks—the rickety wooden Observatory building was strapped and buckled to the summit by heavy chains draped across the roof. But on the day of the Big Wind, the chains had not yet been put to the test. No one knew what was coming.

On the morning of April 12, the youngest member of the crew, a twenty-six-year-old engineer named Wendell Stephenson, walked outside to de-ice the instruments with a hammer. Ice had crusted over the anemometer and the wind vanes, resulting in poor readings.

As soon as he stepped out the door, Stephenson's ears were plugged by the roar of wind; he couldn't hear his own voice even if he screamed. Wind thundered against the rocks like giant kettledrums and howled like wolves.

Stephenson climbed the ladder to the tower, but a 160-mile-per-hour gust raced out of the southeast and pinned him to the wall. He could not climb up—or fall down. "If I'd known how strong the wind was, I'd never have gone out there," he said afterward. As it was, he barely managed to crawl back inside.

A few hours later, when the storm raged to ever greater intensity, the crew watched the walls of their little wooden shack bulge inward; each strong gust pounded the walls like a giant mallet. Would the building stay put? Or would the wind rip open the walls and fling them off the summit?

Later that night, Chief Observer Sal Pagliuca climbed outside to de-ice the instruments again. In the logbook he wrote: "I hammered with all my strength, but I doubt if the strength of Polyphemus could move a sledgehammer in a 200-miles-per-hour breeze."

Meanwhile, downstairs, using a stopwatch and timing the click of their anemometer, the four men calculated a record wind speed of 231 miles per hour. "Our first thought was, will they believe it?" they wrote in the logbook later that night.

Fortunately, the anemometer and stopwatch were tested and proved true, and a new wind speed was added to the record books. It remains unbroken to this day; Mount Washington's claim to the world's worst weather remains unchallenged.

Little Big Wind

The bigger they are, the harder they fall. At least, that was the case on July 20, 1996, when a record-breaking (and bone-breaking) 154-mile-per-hour gust of wind struck the summit of Mount Washington. The gale ripped apart buildings and scooped up bricks, small boulders, hikers, and anything else in its path.

For a three-hour stretch in the afternoon, winds averaged 120 miles per hour, with frequent higher gusts above 140 miles per hour. Ferocious fingers of wind ripped loose a half-dozen cement tiles on the observation deck of the Sherman Adams Summit Building and flung them partway across the peak.

Fortunately, no one was hurt—probably because no one with an ounce of sense dared to visit the summit. The Observatory building itself suffered the worst blow. "Several stone pavers on the deck were lifted out of their slots and deposited several feet away," said Observer Steve Piotrow. "Each eighty-pound block landed on the roof with a reverberating thud."

The savage summer gust of 1996 smashed a sixty-three-year-old record wind for July (the old record of 110 miles per hour was set in 1933). No higher wind speed has ever been recorded on the Rockpile during the months of June, July, or August.

For foul-weather fans, a quick glance at wind statistics throughout the year highlights the mountain's appeal:

	Average wind speed	Highest gust recorded
January	46.3 mph	173 mph
February	44.5	166
March	41.6	180
April	36.1	231
May	29.7	164
June	27.7	136
July	25.3	154
August	25.1	142
September	29.1	174
October	33.8	161
November	39.7	163
December	44.9	178

What is the difference between miles per hour and knots?

When reporting wind data to the National Weather Service, the Mount Washington Observatory records speeds in knots rather than miles per hour. A knot is a unit of speed: one nautical mile per hour, which is equal to 1.15 miles per hour. (Officially, a nautical mile is the length of one minute of longitude at the Earth's equator.)

Knots are typically used to measure the speed of ships or aircraft. In the days of wooden sailing vessels, sailors estimated their speed across the water using knotted ropes. They tied a rope to a large "float," or chunk of wood, dumped the float overboard from the moving ship, and then counted the knots as the rope slipped through their hands. Today, of course, our measurements are more precise.

Knots are a familiar unit on television newscasts up and down the coast, particularly during marine weather forecasts.

It pays to remember that the force of wind is not the same as its speed. The force of wind increases geometrically. A fifty-mile-per-hour gust is not simply twice as strong as a twenty-five-mile-per-hour wind—it's four times as strong!

What makes wind blow? Air molecules flow from areas of high pressure to areas of low pressure. High pressure is where the atmosphere has the most "weight." It seems hard to believe, since we are so used to it, but an average of 14.7 pounds of air (per square inch) press down on our shoulders every second of our lives. That's the weight of hundreds of miles of air molecules stacked up to the sky.

Actually, the higher you go the less the atmosphere weighs, since less air is above you. On Mount Washington, at 6,288 feet above sea level, we feel only 11.7 pounds per square inch. And on Mount Everest, the tallest mountain in the world at 29,028 feet, only about five pounds of air settle on each weary climber's shoulders.

Mount Everest stands near the very top of the troposphere, the breathable lower layer of our atmosphere. The weight of hundreds of miles of air—most of it too thin to breathe—presses down on the troposphere and holds it close to the Earth's surface. Most of the clouds, wind, and storms we think of as weather occur only in the bottom seven miles of the atmosphere.

Oddly enough, no one thought much about the atmosphere until just a few centuries ago. When an ancient Greek scientist named Hero first suggested that air was a substance and had weight, he was laughed at. The idea that "atmospheric pressure"—a fancy term for the weight of air—could be used to predict storms didn't appear until the seventeenth century, when an Italian physicist named Evangelista Torricelli invented the barometer.

To picture how wind flows, imagine a crowd of people jammed into an elevator, standing so close together that their elbows jostle. As soon as the door opens they rush outside, where they have more space. Air molecules behave the same way; they flow from high pressure to low pressure, essentially looking for elbow room.

Wind is air running "downhill" from high to low pressure, spreading out as it goes. The greater the difference in pressure between two regions, the faster the wind blows.

Look closely at a weather map next time you watch the forecast. If an **H**, or high-pressure system, sits close to a big **L**, or low-pressure area, you know that strong wind is on the way. Winds grow stronger and faster when high and low pressure systems move close together.

Since water vapor suspended in the form of clouds makes the atmospheric pressure drop, meteorologists learned that a dip in the barometer often meant a coming storm. So if you hear the words "rapidly falling barometer" in the forecast, it's time to break out your umbrella; low pressure means storms.

Why is Mount Washington so windy? By a strange coincidence, Mount Washington sits at the crossroads of three major storm tracks: the Atlantic Coast, the Ohio River valley, and the line of the Great Lakes. Air masses passing along the three tracks scoop up moisture from these large bodies of water, forming storm clouds that later wring themselves dry over the hills of New England. Another source of wind on Mount Washington is a process called the Bernoulli effect. The mountain "squeezes" wind between the summit and a "lid" in the atmosphere called the tropopause. If you have ever stuck your thumb over the end of a garden hose, you know that constricting the opening makes the water shoot faster. Mount Washington has the same effect—the peak juts above the valley like a giant thumb and makes the wind roar.

> **Sawdust from the Logbook**
>
> *"Century Club, baby! Steve conquers a 125-mph gust and trudges around the observation deck. Mike was really close until he got winded. Meanwhile, our crazy cat Nin jumps up on the weather desk about 6,000 times."*

If you wonder what it feels like to try to stand upright in a hurricane-force wind, just ask the folks at the Observatory. A videotape there offers hours of entertainment, showing people blowing like tumbleweeds across the observation deck. One tape shows a meteorologist slapped away from the door by an invisible paw of wind. To get back, he inches forward but makes no headway. For twenty minutes he flounders on the deck and gets nowhere, like a salmon trying to swim up a waterfall. Someone jokes: "And we never saw Pete again." On camera, the man shrinks into a ball and spins off the screen, lost in fog.

"I was picked up and thrown across the deck like a human hovercraft," Pete said later. To stop his tumble across the summit, he dragged his hands on the ground for a hundred feet—and ruined a good pair of gloves in the process.

Walking—or even crawling—against hurricane-force winds is so difficult because the force of wind increases geometrically. For example, a Class 1 hurricane (winds of 74 miles per hour or greater) is strong enough to rip up a tree like a weed and toss its trunk through a roof. A Class 5 hurricane (above 150 miles per hour) isn't simply twice as strong, it's four times as strong! Imagine trying to stand up while Niagara Falls pours down on your back, and you'll get some idea of the true power of wind. How Sal Pagliuca managed to hold on to a ladder and climb up to the roof in the world record 231-mile-per-hour wind, we'll never know.

FOG

On Mount Washington, the sun is a rare sight in any season. Sometimes a week passes, and all we see is a pale white orb, drowned in deep fog. Three hundred days per year the summit pokes through the clouds, wrapping the rocks in a sheet of mist. Although,

> ### Sawdust from the Logbook
> #### June
> *"Where's the butter knife, we need to cut through this fog. Visibility is down to 25 feet. A couple of lightning crashes sound like they directly hit the tower."*

on a clear day, it's possible to see a hundred miles to the rolling blue waves of the Atlantic, on a foggy day it's hard enough to see your own shoelaces.

What is fog? Fog is a cloud on the ground. Suspended in the air, each particle of fog is a tiny droplet of water less than 0.0006 of an inch in diameter. (To picture how small this really is, take a ruler, a pair of scissors, and a piece of string. Measure a one-inch length of string and try to cut it into ten equal-sized pieces. That's hard enough. But now, you must cut each individual piece a thousand times more—an impossible task.) By comparison, a typical raindrop is .08 inch in diameter, more than a hundred times larger. To compare the sizes of a raindrop to a "fogdrop," think of a basketball next to a pea.

Fog floats in the air; it is not heavy enough to fall like drizzle or rain. Fog (and clouds) form when the air cools to its dew point and becomes saturated with water. Air has a "holding capacity" for water vapor. When the air is "full," at 100 percent relative humidity, the water vapor condenses and fog appears.

Fog is really just an ocean of tiny water droplets afloat in the air. If we could somehow shove all this fog into a compression tank and squeeze it, we could wring out enough water or snow to fill a lake. Clouds appear light and airy, afloat in the sky like clumps of white wool. But clouds do have weight. If you could wring dry a typical cumulus cloud, you would end up with thousands of pounds of water. Even without clouds or fog, the air is still full of moisture, especially on a hot, humid day. All across the planet, some 200 billion tons of water vapor evaporate off the ocean every hour. Later, some of that moisture condenses in the form of clouds and falls as rain or snow.

Not all fog is alike. Ground fog, radiation fog, and sea fog are just a few of many types of fog. Sometimes fog is wet, so wet you think you could practically swim the backstroke through the air. Other times it is relatively dry and thin. In particularly cold regions, where the mercury huddles in the bottom of the thermometer, ice fog can appear. Ice fog is composed of tiny ice particles, unlike normal fog, which is tiny water droplets suspended in the air. Ice fog usually forms at temperatures of −20°F or colder and does not produce rime, which is soft, crumbly ice.

I remember a cold, wet day in June, when billows of fog fluttered in the breeze. Visibility on the summit dropped to less than fifty feet, erasing the distant hills. Hikers who strayed too far from the trail quickly vanished in the mist. Around noontime, a single weary backpacker stumbled through the door of the Sherman Adams summit building and shook raindrops off the sleeves of his parka. A puddle oozed across the floor. The man looked for a ranger, walked over to introduce himself, and then asked, out-of-breath, "Is this the bottom?"

LIGHTNING AND THUNDER

Lightning is no stranger here; the radio towers perched on the peaks are frequent targets. Thunderstorms sometimes ignite them like giant metal candles.

Down in the kitchen on a summer night, the Observatory crew heard the wind surge and growl. A hiss of air whistled through the tower door.

"Is the three-cup down?" asked Ken Rancourt, our research director. Outside, the winds were gusting to fifty miles per hour, strong enough to break twigs off trees. Our fragile three-cup anemometer (used to measure low wind speeds) was unlikely to survive in such strong winds.

No one remembered taking down the three-cup. "It's probably blown away to Conway by now," said Ken.

Since I was on duty, the chore of rescuing the anemometer fell to me.

LYNNE HOST

I put down my fork next to a half-finished slice of eggplant parmesan and ran upstairs.

When I pushed open the door at the top of the tower, a spittle of rain struck my face. My flashlight cut a long yellow beam in the fog; I wielded it like a sword, dissecting the night. My foot splashed in a puddle on the parapet.

Off to one side, an unexpected light blinked on and off. But when I turned to look, the sky was black and empty. "Was it lightning?" I wondered. No storm was expected that night, and I heard no thunder, just the hum of the wind. Perhaps all I saw was the glow of my flashlight on the watery walls.

Up top, the three-cup spun in a frenzy, too fast to see. It hummed like an angry bee and barely registered as a blur in my flashlight beam. I reached up to pull it down . . .

Abruptly, just inches overhead, the sky burst into flame as ribbons of electricity sizzled along the eastern skyline, igniting the Maine border for a hundred miles. A sudden tingle of fear lifted the hairs on my arms. Mount Washington seemed to be poking into the very heart of a thunderstorm! What a predicament: to be standing on the highest point in New England, clutching a metal anemometer, while forks of lightning speared the sky!

Rain trickled down my face; I wiped the water away with a sleeve. I groped for the metal nut that holds the three-cup in place, but my hand slipped on the slick, wet surface; no matter how much I turned, it would not come loose. The sky shook with thunder, as if to say, "This is your last warning!"

Cloud-to-cloud lightning flickered directly above me. Sheets of white electricity snapped in the fog. At last I pulled the nut free, snatched the suddenly quiet three-cup, and ran. I slipped off the last rung of the ladder and end up squat in a puddle. Then, at last, I was safe inside.

My legs felt as if the bones had been drained of marrow, seeming too weak to support my weight. For a second, I just leaned against the wall of two-foot-thick reinforced concrete, regaining my equilibrium while the unexpected storm raged outside.

Does a lightning bolt shoot up or down? To the naked eye, lightning appears to droop from the sky like a fiery vine; each string of electricity dangles off the bottom edge of a cloud. The ancient Greeks imagined Zeus sitting in his throne high on Mount Olympus, hurling lightning down at his enemies.

Actually, what we *see* as lightning is a phenomenon called the return stroke, a sudden surge of positive energy traveling *up* from the ground. But the initial, deadly bolt of lightning is invisible, a stealthy strip of negative energy dropping from the clouds. This "invisible lightning" precedes the brightly lit return stroke by just a fraction of a second.

> ### Sawdust from the Logbook
> ### *August 14, 1988*
> *"Heavy rain and spectacular t-storms kept tourism low. Few visitors, except for the toad who hopped inside."*
> ### *August 15, 1988*
> *"That crazy toad was found this evening in the bottom of the tower. The west wind has blown in an inch or so of rain to make it just right for a toad. On Mount Washington? We took plenty of pictures so the other shift would believe us."*

Can we tell how far away a lightning storm is? Lightning and thunder occur at the same time, but because light travels so much faster than sound, we see lightning a few seconds before we hear thunder. Light reaches our eyes at the astonishing speed of 186,000 miles per second. But sound waves are sluggish; they must plod through the atmosphere at a "mere" 980 feet per second. (This is an average speed; variations in temperature and air density can affect the speed of sound.)

Sound waves travel one mile in about five seconds. To determine how far away the lightning flash occurred, start to count as soon as you see it strike. If you hear thunder two or three seconds later, the lightning strike was only half a mile away. Ten seconds later, two miles away.

Thunder "grumbles" because the sound reaches us at slightly different times from varying points up and down the lightning bolt. Thunder that originates close to the ground will reach us sooner than thunder high in the sky.

What causes thunder? Lightning is hot: nearly 50,000°F, hotter than the surface of the sun. A lightning bolt heats the fluid air around it and causes it to expand. Heated, agitated air scatters in all directions, but quickly encounters cooler air and cools back to normal temperatures. As it cools, the air contracts and "claps" back together. We hear this clap as thunder.

ON THE BRIGHTER DAYS . . .

Fortunately, there is more weather in Mother Nature's kitchen than pea-soup fog and killer winds. She occasionally cooks up bright days and clear nights. One entry in the logbook shows the weather's good side: "April 10, 1997. Celestial madness!!! Today was one of those days that reminds us why we're here. We set a record cold temperature of –8°F in the morning, had a peak wind gust of 108 mph a few hours later, enjoyed 100-mile visibility in the afternoon, and were treated to a once-in-a-lifetime celestial display consisting of the Hale-Bopp comet, a dazzling curtain of aurora borealis, a crescent moon, and shooting stars after sunset." Our rare clear-sky days give the Observatory summit dwellers treasured opportunities to witness a variety of spectacular and colorful phenomena.

Sunsets paint the clouds with brilliant reds and oranges. Clouds churn in the sky like flames, ignited by the sun. More clouds stampede across the valleys below, and the higher summits poke through to the sky like islands in the sea. I stare at the first glimmers of twilight from the top of the tower, my hair rustled by a light wind. The orange circle of the sun hangs over the hills, dripping fiery drops into a chasm below the horizon. The earth seems to roll faster as night nears; the sun and the mountains trapped below it stampede deep into the shadows. Quickly, the sun is squashed into an oval against the distant hills of New York.

In the valleys, constellations of brightly lit lakes sparkle and wink off one by one. Soon the sun is just a puddle of light, a distant lake of fire tucked between two mountains. Night closes in. Finally, the sun sits in a groove of mountains, a dull red coal emitting its last flicker. Just before it dies, as the last lip of fire licks the horizon, we see a colorful glow—the so-called green flash.

"There it goes—*poof*—just like that," says a ranger, leaning against the tower's parapet. "With any luck it'll be back again tomorrow," he adds.

What makes a rainbow?

During April showers—or any other time of year when it rains—arcs of color may curve across the sky. A rainbow appears whenever sunlight slices through falling raindrops, splintering into many colors in the process. Distant raindrops act just like a prism.

Sunlight "bends" when it passes through water. To see how water can bend light, simply stick a pencil in a clear glass of water and peer inside. The pencil will appear to break at the point where it enters the water.

What does all this have to do with rainbows? Just this—sunlight appears white, but it is actually a jumbled mix of many colors, and different colors of light bend to different degrees. For instance, red light bends in water slightly more than orange light, just as orange light bends more than green. So in a sense, rays of sunlight that pass through a prism (or through a raindrop) "line up" in a particular order. All these colors make up the spectrum.

School children are taught to remember the colors of the spectrum by reciting a name: "Roy G. Biv" (red, orange, yellow, green, blue, indigo, and violet). Each color is made up of light at different wavelengths. Red light has the longest wavelength, and violet has the shortest. Ultraviolet light, which causes sunburns, has an even shorter wavelength and is not visible to the human eye.

You are most likely to spot a rainbow early in the morning or late in the afternoon, when the sun is low in the sky. To increase the chances of seeing one, stand with the sun at your back shortly after a rain shower has ended (rain must still be falling nearby). Some of the sun's rays will enter a raindrop, bounce off the back of the drop, and be reflected into your eyes. Raindrops at different angles from you reflect different colors. That creates the spectacle of the rainbow.

Turn your head to take a step forward, and you will see a "new" rainbow, formed from a different set of raindrops. In fact, two people can stand right next to each other and admire the colors of a rainbow in the sky, but they will actually be looking at different water droplets and different rainbows!

Rainbows form as a circle around a point in the sky. Because of the horizon, we see an arc, a portion of that circle.

What is the green flash? At dusk on a clear night, the last sliver of sun will glow a pale green as it dips below the horizon. The sun's light is being refracted, or bent, in the atmosphere, split into many colors, like light through a prism. For a brief instant, we see the green segment of the spectrum.

The flash is best seen through binoculars (but be careful not to look until the very last sliver of the sun sinks below the horizon; it is dangerous to look directly at the sun). The effect only lasts for a pale second, and can only be seen in a clear sky, either from a mountaintop or looking across a flat surface like the ocean. Of course, since Mount Washington has its nose in the clouds three hundred days a year, seeing the green flash at sunset is a rare treat for the Observatory crew.

Clear nights sometimes reveal the awe-inspiring aurora borealis—the northern lights—rippling in the sky behind Mount Jefferson.

What causes the northern lights? These bright ribbons of light dancing like ghosts in the sky are caused by charged particles from the sun mingling with our atmosphere. Frequent storms on the sun's surface spit out high-energy particles called ions, which fly into outer space. As the ions approach earth, our planet's magnetic field pulls them toward the poles. High-energy ions "jump-start" molecules in the atmosphere, causing them to emit light. Most of our atmosphere is made of nitrogen, which turns a red or violet color, and oxygen, which can glow either red or green. This gives the aurora it's colors (though, seen from a distance, it often appears only a dull white).

All the action happens seventy miles or higher above the earth's surface, far above the breathable lower portion of our atmosphere. Over the Arctic Circle, aurora borealis can be seen nearly every clear night. Here in New England, much farther from the north pole, the phenomenon is not quite so common.

In addition to colorful rainbows, northern lights, and some truly memorable sunsets, the members of the Mount Washington Observatory crew are treated to a bird's-eye view of the most spectacular fall foliage in the world. Although no autumn leaves blow across the stark world above timberline, where no trees can survive the cruel whip of wind, a glimpse from the

Observatory tower down into the ravines and the lower slopes reveals a swath of golden leaves. At the foot of Mount Washington lies a canopy of maples, birches, and green pine trees, laced together by needles and twigs. The forest fits against the base of the mountain like a snug wooden shoe.

What colors autumn leaves? Weather plays a role in how bright the autumn leaves will be. A rainy summer season nourishes the cells that provide pigment, or color, but a drought in summer is bad news. If you have ever forgotten to water a houseplant, you know it turns a sickly pale yellow. Trees in the wild behave much the same way. Pigments in the leaves are darker and richer when the trees have had more rainwater to drink.

Actually, the red and yellow pigments that appear in autumn leaves are there all the time, but in summer they are masked by green chlorophyll cells. When the chlorophyll fades during the short days and cold nights of fall, the leaves expose a prism of bright colors underneath the green. Chlorophyll is the basis of photosynthesis, the process by which leaves sip energy from sunlight. Essentially, a chlorophyll molecule snatches hold of a ray of sunlight and converts it to food.

In summer, chlorophyll is the dominant color of leaves: green. When the green color fades in autumn, a pigment called carotene paints some leaves orange. Xanthophyll creates yellow, while anthocyanins turn other leaves deep red and purple.

SOLID WATER

The average temperature at the summit of Mount Washington in September is 34.6 degrees, but in October the air chills to an average of 24.2, well below freezing. And that means it is time for rime, snow flurries, and freezing rain as we leave summer behind and move into the colder seasons. Officially, the meteorological winter begins on December 1 (the "calendar" winter

> **Sawdust from the Logbook**
> ***December 4, 1988***
>
> *"Dana goes out on the roof in sneakers to measure the rods. The 80-mph winds blow him to the rotunda with his sneakers acting like skis on the icy ground. He throws himself flat and must crawl back for lack of traction. Quite an adventure!"*

starts on the winter solstice, December 21). But sometimes it feels as though winter lasts from September all the way through May. Eleven inches of snow typically fall in May.

What is freezing rain? Rain that falls as a liquid but freezes on impact is called freezing rain, designated by the abbreviation ZR or FZRA on the hourly weather reports compiled by the Observatory staff. It might seem strange that liquid water can fall when the air temperature is below 32°F, but that's exactly what happens. The liquid actually cools to below freezing, and as soon as it hits the Observatory tower or the rocks, it solidifies into a treacherously slippery sheet of ice.

Glaze ice versus rime ice. Glaze ice is like glass—hard, clear, and slippery. It is formed by the splatter of freezing rain or freezing drizzle. Rime, on the other hand, is feathery thin, soft, and easily crumbled.

Rime forms from fog. With the summit of Mount Washington frequently in the fog, supercooled cloud droplets freeze on contact with anything solid: rocks, walls, people—and scientific instruments. Rime is basically a tiny bubble of cold air wrapped in ice. Spears of rime grow into the wind, and it's not uncommon to have a six-foot-long shaft of rime groping over the edge of a tower, like the giant, hairy arm of a Yeti (an Abominable Snowman), reaching down to the ground below.

De-icing the instruments is an ongoing task for the Observatory crew. Goggles protect eyes from flying ice chunks.

One of the Observatory's many research projects is to measure the accumulation of ice on a device called a multicylinder. From this data, run through a computer, we can study the size and formation of cloud droplets.

Both rime and glaze ice encase the instruments and must constantly be hammered off to ensure accurate readings. Gauges and anemometers are not accurate if encased in rime, so the crew at the Mount Washington Observatory works up a sweat hammering the ice off the tower. It was rime ice on the anemometer that compelled Sal Pagliuca to stand atop the tower in a two-hundred-mile-per-hour wind in 1934.

It comes as no surprise that the summits of the White Mountains see plenty of snow. A typical December dumps 43 inches of snow on the summit, though in 1968, 103.7 inches fell in that month alone. In fact, the winter of 1968–69 was the snowiest one on record, with 566 inches all told.

Let's compare a "real" winter to a winter in Caribou, Maine, a town where people are said to spend more time driving snowmobiles than cars. For good measure, we'll throw in statistics from Boston, as well. Here are how the numbers add up for February 1969, one of the snowiest months in New England history.

Here is how Mount Washington Weather stacks up against Boston and Caribou all year-round.

February 1969	Mt. Washington	Caribou	Boston
Average temperature	8.2°F	17.7°F	29.7°F
High temperature	34°F	43°F	40°F
Low temperature	−25°F	−20°F	12°F
Snow accumulation	172.8"	29.7"	41.3"
Greatest 24-hr snowfall	49.3"	12.8"	13.7"
	Mt. Washington	Caribou	Boston
Average annual temp.	26.5°F	38.8°F	51.5°F
All-time high temperature	72°F	96°F	104°F
All-time low temperature	−47°F	−41°F	−12°F
Average wind speed	35.3 mph	11.2 mph	12.5 mph
Highest wind speed	231 mph	76 mph	76 mph
Average yearly snowfall	255.3"	110"	40"
Greatest annual snowfall	566.4"	181"	108"

What makes it cold, anyway? Cold, or heat, is a matter of kinetic energy, a measure of how fast atoms and molecules move. Heat things up, and molecules move faster. In the cold blackness of outer space, the temperature comes very close to absolute zero, at which point even the innards of an atom shrivel up and freeze. Absolute zero is −459.67°F. At such a temperature, nothing moves at all.

A good example of energy in motion is an Observatory crew member shooting down the mountain on a sled. What a way to commute home from work! The sledder has kinetic energy when he is in motion, but potential energy when perched at the top, waiting for a shove on the back to get him moving. ("A sledder has the potential to slip and break his neck, hence, potential energy," jokes an Observer.)

IT COULD BE WORSE . . .

Weather in the North Country is always unpredictable. During the summer months—July and August—kaleidoscopes of clouds reel overhead, depositing rain, hail, fog, and drops of sunlight in equal measure. In fall and winter, frost, sleet, and snow are the norm.

"You have winter nine months a year!" groans a friend of mine from Seattle, peeking out from under her mandatory umbrella. And I confess, it's true; in some places, like the bowl of Tuckerman Ravine, the snow sea-

Measuring temperature

Different parts of the world use different scales to measure temperature. The familiar Fahrenheit scale, widely used in the United States, was invented by Gabriel Fahrenheit in 1714. Most of the rest of the world, including our neighbors in Canada, use the centigrade, or Celsius, scale, which was invented by Anders Celsius in 1742.

In the centigrade scale, water boils at 100 and freezes at 0. In Fahrenheit the temperatures are 212 and 32, respectively. If the temperature drops far enough, the two scales meet at −40°.

son lasts until late July. But it wasn't always so; one year, summer never came at all.

In 1816, drought and unseasonable cold tormented farmers throughout the Northeast. Winter stubbornly refused to yield to spring. At the same time, to everyone's dismay, a mysterious black spot appeared on the sun. Swarms of smaller spots could also be seen, plainly visible to the naked eye. Clearly something was wrong.

Were celestial apparitions to blame for a never-ending season of snow and cold? Many thought so, and panicked. Down in Massachusetts, one amateur astronomer claimed to have seen a sunspot explode before his eyes. "The appearance was that of a piece of ice which, when dashed on a frozen pond, breaks to pieces, and slides in every direction."

Such apocalyptic visions did little to soothe peoples' fears. At dawn and dusk, the life-giving sun glowed a pale, sickly orange, blotted with spots, as if it had caught a pox. To make matters worse, snow squalls struck northern New England in May, June, and July, while killing frosts damaged or destroyed crops in the Berkshires and Connecticut. Was the sun ill, people wondered? Were blemishes on the sun's surface preventing light and heat from reaching the earth?

Actually, the grim weather of 1816 is now blamed on large quantities of dust in the atmosphere, spewed from a volcanic eruption in faraway Indonesia the year before. (The eruption of Mount St. Helens in 1980 also filled the sky with volcanic ash, but to a much lesser degree.)

Whatever effects the sunspot activity also may have had on the climate is still uncertain, but the dust from the 1815 explosion of Mount Tambora certainly dimmed the sun, making its dark spots easier to see. Many people who had never noticed sunspots before suddenly became aware of them, while astronomers pondered possible relationships between sunspot activity and peculiarities in the weather.

We know today that sunspots are merely large cool regions of the sun's photosphere, not portents of impending doom. In 1816, laymen knew nothing about solar mechanics, and astronomers knew little more.

With typical Yankee humor, a newspaper column poked fun at the raging debate: "The PHENOMENON which has excited so much astonishment . . . is a large PUMPKIN." This theory about sunspots and cold weather was advanced by a "Mr. Philander Sarcasm" in newspapers around the country. As Mr. Sarcasm explained, the giant solar pumpkin dangled from a vine "of sufficient length to reach below the circumnambient atmosphere of the sun" and thus be visible from Earth. He added, "It will be visible every revolution of the Sun, until it is gathered."

Apparently someone harvested the celestial pumpkin in late autumn. By 1817, sunspot activity decreased significantly, volcanic dust started to dissipate, and the weather returned to what passes for normal in New England.

Looking south from Mount Washington to Mount Monroe.

Living on the Rockpile–
"The Highest Paying Jobs in New England"

Nature cycles through the seasons on a regular basis, though here on the Rockpile it sometimes feels as if we experience the best—and worst—of all four seasons in a single day. Despite the variability of the weather, each season does bring a comfortable routine to the Observatory.

In summer, for example, the summit crew and state park rangers share the peak with a quarter of a million hikers, backpackers, and sightseers. Each morning, the Cog Railway chugs up the steep slopes like the Little Engine that Could.

Winter brings an entirely new set of responsibilities and expectations. The doors of the state park building and gift shop are sealed from late October till mid-May; savage weather soon buries the Cog Railway tracks under hillocks of drifting snow. Winter winds are powerful enough to push snow through cracks in doorways, so the Observatory crew must occasionally shovel snowdrifts *inside* the Mount Washington Museum.

As October edges into November and the full force of winter hits the Rockpile, transportation on shift-change day becomes a weekly challenge. Ridges of snow and layers of ice cause the Observatory's van to slip and slide. Soon a four-

The Observatory's Sno-Cat transports *crew members to the summit. On a good day the eight-mile trip takes an hour and a half; in a snowstorm it can take as long as five hours. Occasionally the driver has no choice but to turn back.*

MOUNT WASHINGTON OBSERVATORY

wheel-drive truck with chains on its tires is the only safe means of reaching the peak. By late December, not even this big vehicle can negotiate the growing snowdrifts.

After that point, a tank-like Sno-Cat is used to plow its way to the summit, a trip that lasts an hour and a half even in the best of circumstances. In foul weather, when visibility is obscured by low clouds, the eight-mile journey can take four hours or even more.

Only a handful of Observers (plus two technicians at the WMTW-TV 8 transmitter building) stay on the summit through the entire winter. Supplies such as fresh food and drinking water are brought up by Sno-Cat each Wednesday. (Tap water for showers and washing dishes is stored in giant holding tanks, located in a deep corner of the Sherman Adams Summit Building.)

Deep winter on the Rockpile is a lonelier, quieter time. In summer, by comparison, dozens of park rangers, Cog Railway engineers, Auto Road drivers, and Appalachian Mountain Club guides also work on the mountain. More than 250,000 visitors and sightseers crowd the slopes and summit each year, mostly on sunny summer weekends.

As the seasons change, so too does life at the top.

SPRING

Winter weather is always prowling the summit of Mount Washington, and sometimes the ice is reluctant to slacken its grip come spring. The aver-

The Century Club

One of the treasured Observatory staff traditions is the Century Club. Membership in the club is limited to individuals who can successfully walk the length of the observation deck and back in winds of 100 miles per hour or more. "If you fall down or blow away, it doesn't count," explains one of the crew. Another rule is, if you disappear, your membership is awarded posthumously. The entire Century Club Membership Roll still falls short of filling one 8½-by-11-inch page.

age overnight low temperature on the mountain is only 5°F in March, with frequent dips below zero. Snow continues to fall with all the intensity of winter. But the thaw is on nonetheless; cold rain finally starts to wash away the rime in April and May.

Deep snowdrifts make it necessary for the Observatory crew to use the Sno-Cat to travel up and down the mountain. On an unusually warm day in March 1992, one meteorologist noted in the Observatory logbook: "Came up today in deep slush and water. At times the Sno-Cat would plow through a four-foot-deep river of slush, with water gushing over the treads."

Sawdust from the Logbook
March 3, 1996

"Mother Nature unleashed a mighty gale, but her fury couldn't stop our feisty, fun-loving Observatory crew from frolicking outside. Alas, the Century Club status we so desperately sought eluded our grasp. (Collective sigh.) Nevertheless, 97-mph winds were enough to hurl one man to the ground and dislodge his hat and goggles. He watched his headgear gleefully skip away in the breeze, never to be seen again."

Later, when a cold front passed through, he wrote: "Snow, snow, snow . . . oh, let it blow." As March edged into April that year, winter conditions still prevailed: "The blizzard wasn't as bad as I expected," reads another entry in the logbook, "but we did have a peak gust of 145 mph. It took quite a bit of work to go outside. The wind knifed right through my jacket, pants, and overmitts. I had snow buildup on the inside of my goggles."

Finally, in April and May, warm breezes melt away half-a-year's worth of snow and ice. Talk about change! Creeks full of cold water gurgle down the rocky mountain slopes and wash the boulders clean. Dark spikes of rock poke up through a roof of melting snow. All across New England, the ground thaws and rivers ripple and surge with the runoff of melting snow. In the valleys, maple branches sprout buds and the first flowers bloom. The air is a gentle breeze, a warm sigh of relief after the cold gusts of February.

On Mount Washington, the average temperature in May is still only 35°F, but that's a steep rise from the chilly 22°F of April and the 13°F typical of March. For the first time in many months, above-freezing tem-

peratures become common—especially in mid-afternoon, when the sun's
hot yellow rays pour down on the rocks.

After a long, icy winter huddled inside the Observatory's concrete walls,
what a relief it is to "dress down" into a mere wool sweater, rather than the usual
combination of heavy parka, face mask, wind pants, and goggles. But not
everyone on the mountaintop is pleased. I once saw a message scribbled in the
pages of the logbook: "Winter disappears overnight. Whoever took away the
snow better bring it back real soon."

Perhaps those grumblers miss the end of sledding season. A delightful
perk of life on the summit is the chance to sled down the mountain. Where
else in the world, aside from an Olympic luge competition, can you enjoy
an uninterrupted eight-mile run? (Unfortunately, the sleds don't work too
well on the trip back up.) You've heard the old saying, "April showers bring

Spring skiing can last well into June in Tuckerman Ravine.
Today's skiers still wend their way to the Headwall
just as these snow enthusiasts did in the 1940s.

May flowers"; on Mount Washington, April flurries bring May worries—and also provide a last chance to play in the snow before the warm breath of summer melts it all away.

It is late May, and a thin layer of hail and ice cakes the ground. With winds gusting to seventy-five miles per hour, a young crew member bundles into a heavy parka and steps outside. The wind whooshes the door out of his hand and slams it shut; a metallic echo shudders through the Sherman Adams summit building. Instantly, fingers of wind snatch his shoulders and fling him away from the door. To stop, he stoops and curls into a ball, dragging his gloves against the ground. Rime ice clings to his hat, and his bright blue jacket turns white with snow, sparkling in the moonlight. Undeterred, the meteorologist tucks a red plastic sled under his arm and hauls it to the edge of the observation deck. Finally, he kneels in the sled, holding out his arms like a ship's spars. Wind puffs up his jacket like a ship's sail and nudges him quickly across the deck. His sleigh ride across the ice ends in a pile of snow a few seconds later.

After a long, brutal winter, the temperature suddenly shoots above freezing. In the minds of the summit crew, a heat wave of 40°F feels just like the Bahamas.

During the warmest days of the spring thaw, meteorologists on Mount Washington start to melt away like snowmen. Spring thaw changes the tasks at hand. Icing-research projects are put in mothballs until the snow flies again. Technicians in the TV-8 transmitter building across the summit emerge from their icy cocoon and stroll across the peak. Far down the slope, bulldozers and plows help the Auto Road crew carve a path through lingering layers of snow and ice.

Opening day for the visitor center is not far away. In May, doors that have been sealed all winter are cracked open in preparation for the summer tourist season. Visitors from southern New England start to climb to the peak, taunting the isolated summit-dwellers with visions of dandelions in the grass. But no dandelions grow in the rocky world above tree line, where the sedges and grasses stay brown until mid-June. Instead, each June, arctic flowers left over from the last ice age suddenly wink open on the peaks. Stranded above timberline, clumps of half-open diapensia blossoms yawn at the sky. Their white petals smile up at the sun.

The reappearance of the sun after endless months of being buried in fog is just one of many changes for weather observers on top of Mount Washington. Since a typical winter dumps more than 255 inches of snow on the mountain, it comes as a bit of a shock when warm, wet water droplets start to plummet from the sky. "What do you call it? Rain?" asks a puzzled mountain meteorologist, scratching his head.

The idea of "unfrozen precipitation" takes a bit of getting used to, but pretty soon we have rainwater up to our ears. When the first downpour or thunderstorm clobbers the mountain, the Observatory watchtower fills with water like a giant canteen. Melting snow dribbles through cracks in the cement, and rainwater gushes down the hatch from the parapet. Inside, the cold cement walls drip and run. "We have heavy rain showers inside the tower," someone shouts. "Time to start building an ark!"

As I climb up the ladder to the parapet, fat drops trickle off the rungs of the ladder and fall with a plunk in a puddle at the bottom. Other drops *splat* against my face. Rainwater mats my hair like a cold shower. And yet, here I am safely inside a building, with a thick concrete roof overhead.

During a spring thunderstorm, the Observatory tower feels like the innards of a submarine, its walls squeezed by the immense pressure of the ocean. Water percolates off the walls, and a constant dripping noise plunks in the background. "Man the lifeboats, start bailing," reads an entry in the logbook. Sometimes it's hard to believe we are more than a mile above sea level. When the highest point in New England starts to flood, you know that spring is here at last.

SUMMER

In summer, icicles finally melt away and drip into the rocks. Fog clears, and boulders studded with glassy minerals start to glitter in the sun.

Summertime is a mix of bustling activity and quiet contemplation on Mount Washington. A thoughtful weather observer wrote in the logbook on

July 7, 1994, "Today was a quiet day on the summit, as fog and rain showers kept most of the visitors home."

Even in summer, fields of tundra grass ripple and writhe in the wind. Icy fingers of wind still poke and prod the boulders above timberline. On average, only an inch of snow falls in June, with just a few flurries in July and August. Unfortunately, many hikers and mountain climbers come unprepared for the possibility of subarctic conditions. They forget that

Sawdust from the Logbook
June 19, 1995
"Oh the heat was practically unbearable today! We broke a record by hitting 67°F. Down at Lakes of the Clouds, a hiker fell on the rocks and badly cut herself. Observatory and State Park folks carried her in a litter to the summit, where she was evacuated to a hospital via the Auto Road."

even in summer, Old Man Winter sometimes sneaks up on the summit and wraps his icy arms around unsuspecting travelers. Accidents and deaths occur in the mountains in all seasons, so the Observatory staff and the state park crew are always on call, cooperating in search-and-rescue operations.

Summer days bring visitors, as sightseers and hikers congregate on the top of Mount Washington. But is there any pity for our poor, windblown summit staff? Each morning on shift-change day, after all the rangers, meteorologists, and other employees battle their way through savage gusts to reach the Sherman Adams summit building, they immediately encounter a barrage of questions, comments, and complaints.

"Do you ever get any moose up here?" a tall man from down-state once asked. He leaned on the countertop with his elbows and pointed to the piles of mica-schist boulders with a thrust of his chin. "Yes, we do get moose above tree line," the ranger answered. "Not often, though." The man paused; his chin drooped. Finally he inquired, "How do you get them up here?"

Workers on the summit—park rangers, gift shop employees, and meteorologists at the Mount Washington Observatory—have compiled a list of odd, amusing, or alarming questions put to them by tourists. The list circulates amid gales of puzzled laughter during off-hours:

"Can I park my car on the roof?"

"Are these mountains above sea level?"

"This is my first time up Mount Washington. What am I supposed to do?"

A young, ponytailed visitor once stepped up to the ranger's desk with an important question: "Do you have a microwave oven?" When the ranger replied in the affirmative, she asked, "Can I use it to dry my boyfriend's pants?"

The most common question is, "Where are all the presidents' faces?" Visitors who have driven to New Hampshire's mountains from afar are never pleased to learn that Mount Rushmore is sixteen-hundred miles away. Mount Washington may be named for our first President, but its stones are not etched with his image.

"Is this the tallest mountain in the state of Washington?" other visitors have asked.

"Do you work for the state of Connecticut?"

"Who runs this place, the state of Vermont?"

"Can we see New Hampshire from here?"

Since Mount Washington lies along the Appalachian Trail, it is occasionally visited by "thru-hikers" on their way from Georgia to Mount Katahdin in northern Maine. Such well-traveled hikers can be identified by sight and (especially) smell, and other "normal" sightseers are often curious about them: "After they hike up the two-thousand-mile-long Appalachian Trail, how do they get back down?"

"Are the trails lit for night hiking?"

From time to time a moose wanders up to the summit.

"Do you have an elevator to the base?"

In the end, of course, Mount Washington will always be most famous for its winds and weather. "Is it always this windy up here?" hikers usually ask.

"You claim that this place has the world's worst weather. I always thought Philadelphia did."

"Is there any danger of this mountain erupting while I'm on it?"

In ancient times, people climbed mountains to ask wise hermits for advice. But today, things are different. Instead of long-bearded gurus, young park rangers and meteorologists inhabit our mountaintops. So visitors should feel free to ask any questions. But remember: up on Mount Washington, at least, the answers really are blowing in the wind.

Summer is a perfect time to hike down to the alpine garden to pick wild blueberries for next morning's pancakes and muffins. And who knows? Like many visitors to Mount Washington, you might meet a bear or a moose along the way.

The first "wild" animal I encountered on the summit was neither a fox nor a moose. Instead, it was a chubby orange beast named Jasper. You won't

Sawdust from the Logbook

Summer 1996

"We've been in the fog pretty much all day, except for an hour right around sunset, which featured some nice colors, beautiful clouds, and a double rainbow on the horizon. Even the fox [a regular visitor to the summit] came out on the observation deck to admire the view. She was very tame and came within ten feet of me, staring at me with her inquisitive, intelligent-looking eyes."

Summer 1994

"Hip hip hooray! The fog's gone away. Low clouds spill over the northern Presidentials and produce a beautiful dark-red sunset. A spectacular star show and ninety-mile visibility entertain us in the evening. Even the fox stops by for a visit."

Summer 1993

Summer 1993. "Big news today is the moose, sighted early afternoon near the lower parking lot, hanging out on a patch of sedge. He was still there at dark. I guess this is moose #3 for the season. Let's hope he's a survivor, though I suppose there are some who'd like to see him in the freezer."

find this mammal listed in any zoology books; he is known to only a few. He lurks in his lair deep below ground, in the living quarters of the Observatory.

I first met Jasper the cat on a chilly evening when westerly winds were whipping across the summit at seventy miles per hour. I stood alone on the mountaintop and watched a dark fist of cloud punch slowly toward the peaks, beaching itself on the rocks. Gray mist splashed on the boulders like ocean spray. As I stumbled through the fog, bullets of hail nipped at my face, and the hood of my jacket flapped like a sail. With each strong gust, the precipitation can that I was carrying squirmed in my arms like an angry cat.

I encountered a truly angry cat back in the shelter of the observatory. Jasper was not a happy animal when I rudely walked in from the cold and picked him up; I even had the nerve to try to pet him. He squirmed and struggled in my arms until I let him go, but graciously accepted a bowl of milk as a peace offering. He even begged pitifully for a second peace offering two minutes later.

"Is Jasper an outdoor cat?" I wondered aloud.

One of the meteorologists laughed. "I wouldn't say that. The only door Jasper waits in front of is the refrigerator's."

For fourteen years, Jasper has survived inside the warm belly of the Mount Washington Observatory while sleet and hail battered the windowpanes and hurricane-force winds rattled the walls. Outside, sheets of icy rain have shattered on the rocks like glass, but a snoozing Jasper has purred through it all.

Like most cats, Jasper is a hunter. One night, he trotted off into the twilight and jogged back with a mouse tucked between his jaws. He deposited

Jasper confronts another summit resident.

his prize in the doorway and ran back for more. By night's end, a row of rodents lay scattered across the observation deck, sorted by size. Everyone was surprised.

"He was stacking them up like cordwood," announced one early riser. We expected the Environmental Protection Agency to show up any minute to declare the American house mouse an endangered species.

The famous, frosty Inga.

What's so odd about an orange tabby cat who lives on top of a mountain and likes to eat asparagus? In Jasper's case, quite a bit. He often flees in terror from children but tolerates adults, so long as they hold him upside down (he hates being held right-side up) and put plenty of milk in his drinking bowl.

For more than a decade, a traumatized Jasper played second fiddle to Inga, the famous calico cat with frosty whiskers. Inga was always the teacher's pet, the spoiled child. A darling of the media, she was "interviewed" by *Cat Fancy* magazine while a jealous Jasper sulked in obscurity.

A picture of an icy Inga is still printed on T-shirts, posters, postcards, and refrigerator magnets that are sold each summer in the Mount Washington Museum gift shop. When Inga passed away in 1993 at age nineteen, her estate generously donated all proceeds from her modeling career to the Observatory.

Sadly, Jasper has enjoyed no such notoriety. While thousands of Inga postcards are shipped to mailboxes all across the continent, poor Jasper lurks in the shadows, far from the public eye. Even worse, a new nemesis named Nin appeared on the scene in 1996, just when Jasper thought he finally had the summit to himself. (Rumors to the contrary, Nin's name is not short for nincompoop—though it should be!) Nin poses for the cameras and purrs in the arms of visiting journalists. He also robs Jasper's food

Sawdust from the Logbook
June 20, 1996
Nin, the incredible hiking cat,
conquers Mount Clay this
morning (meower power).
Humans Matt and Jake tag along.

bowl when the older cat isn't looking.

Jasper, patient as always, endures. The only legacy of this big, shy, but basically friendly cat is likely to be a clump of orange furballs left behind on the living room rug.

The Mount Washington Observatory has a legacy of wild winds, eccentric cats (and people), and famous foods. And at no time is the culinary expertise of our meteorologists more on display than in summer. The State Park rangers live just a few steps away, and their presence inspires "cook-offs" with the Observatory crew.

In the Observatory logbook, one late-summer entry reads: "Plenty of ice outside, but down in the museum it's like July again—at least in terms of sales. Hundreds of hikers scramble to the summit for the weekend, and a good portion of them are folks staying for dinner. Yes, tonight is the annual Guadalajara night! Thirty-six people squeeze around three tables. After dinner, they stagger upstairs to look at the stars. Bodies scattered everywhere by night's end."

Guadalajara night is the high point and finale of the summer culinary season on Mount Washington. "The tradition began one night with a single pitcher of margaritas," explains the Observatory's long-time executive director, Guy Gosselin. "They were deemed 'the best margaritas north of Guadalajara,' and the night soon blossomed into a full-blown Mexican feast." This annual "holiday" serves up an introduction to the hot, spicy foods that will dominate Observatory meals during the upcoming winter season.

Around the Observatory dinner table, hordes of hungry meteorologists, geologists, park rangers, and invited guests sample the finest food available a mile above the sea. "The weather might be cold," says a guest, helping himself to a generous portion of spicy rice and beans, "but the food sure is hot."

A sampling of this fiery fare is included in the "Recipes" chapter beginning on page 67.

FALL

"It's coat season out there," complains a tall, bearded man bundled up like an Eskimo in a heavy parka, but still shivering with cold. With a shaky arm, he yanks open the door to the Observatory and staggers back outside, nudged by a sudden gust of wind. His coat drips with cold rain, and a crust of glaze ice soon clings to his hat. Needles of ice encase his eyelids and droop off the reddish hairs in his beard. Behind him, a hurricane-force breeze slams the door shut with a harsh metallic clang.

I step outside to see this remarkable weather for myself. After all, just yesterday there were sunbathers on the roof. Can the seasons change so quickly?

You bet they can. Snow and ice can turn to sunshine in a matter of minutes—and turn back again. Walking across the observation deck, I watch as the last stars wink out one by one in the early morning sky. A fresh autumn wind blows raw against my face. I rub my hands for warmth, wishing I had worn gloves.

At six a.m., deep below the horizon, the sun leaks a trickle of dawn onto the sky. The first glint of golden light wafts on the breeze like the scent of honey from a faraway tree, but no warmth comes with it. I can feel goose bumps prickle on my skin. A fresh sheet of ice cracks under my boots with

MOUNT WASHINGTON OBSERVATORY

Skiers pose beside the Mount Washington Cog Railway engine in autumn.

every step, and the western half of the sky oozes with fog. Low stratocumulus clouds wash up over the summit from time to time, splashing the rocks with mist. Despite a brief break in the clouds at sunrise, foul weather quickly returns.

Overhead, the sky hangs shaggy and low. Nimbostratus clouds sit in dark gray lumps, dangling precariously above the summit like stalactites about to break loose and fall. Such clouds always produce a steady rain or snow. Scattered clumps of fog often materialize just below the main base of the cloud as falling rain and moisture condense. These little islands of fog are called scud clouds.

Why do we have seasons in the first place?

The earth spins on its axis like a wobbly top, as first the North Pole and then the South Pole take turns basking in the sun. In December, the South Pole enjoys one long, endless day. Up at the North Pole, at the same time, the sun never rises at all, keeping the ice cap in perpetual darkness all winter long.

Ironically, summer in the Northern Hemisphere is the season when we are farthest from the sun. Since the Earth's orbit is not quite a perfect circle, in July we fly a little bit deeper into the cold reaches of outer space.

Why does the land heat up when we "walk away" from the sun, our only source of heat? After all, no one expects to get warmer by moving away from the fireplace in a cold room.

It turns out that our distance from the sun (give or take a few million miles) has little effect. But since days are longer than nights during the summer, we spend more hours heating up than we do cooling down. To further intensify the heat, the sun hangs higher in the sky in summer, so its warm rays grow more intense.

A slight tilt in the Earth's axis makes the seasons wax and wane. That is all that separates the warm breezes of summer from the icy howls of winter.

All morning, snow pours from the sky in fat flakes, set aswirl by the wind. Though the calendar says it is only early September, winter appears to have arrived in full force. When I retreat to the weather room, I see a note in the logbook, jotted down in blue ink: "Start your Christmas Shopping, the season's first snow fell today." I glance at the thermograph and read a temperature of only 28°F, just a few degrees south of the freezing mark. In the background, I hear a crew member usher in the winter season by whistling, "Let it snow, let it snow, let it snow."

Apparently winter is in a hurry this year. It forgot to wait for fall.

"When summer birds take their flight, summer goes with them" is an old gem of weather folklore. Our ancestors watched birds fly south each autumn, shortly before the first frosts. They learned that the migration of birds was an omen, indicating a time when summer's warm breezes gave way to the cold embrace of winter.

On Mount Washington, the visitors disappear and migrate south long before the birds do. Snowstorms and cold drive away most tourists to more

Stranded on the summit on October 8, 1988,
this cog-railway locomotive was a casualty of one of the earliest and longest
stretches of bad weather in recent memory.

comfortable climates. The State Park seals its doors, and the Auto Road and Cog Railway close up shop for the season. Any hardy hikers and skiers who stay on the peaks must put away their summer hiking boots and dig out ice axes, crampons, and whatever gear gives them a solid foothold on the ice.

In the Presidential Range, the switch from summer to winter gives little warning. Autumn is just a short, colorful prelude to winter. High atop the White Mountains, on cold September days, Old Man Winter scouts around the rocks and ravines, searching for good spots for avalanches. He reaches deep into his pockets and sprinkles a little snow on the peaks. If you are hiking in autumn, it pays to come prepared. After a virtually snow-free summer, Mount Washington can wake up under a blanket of snow at any time from late August to mid-September.

The season's first snow shower usually falls on Mount Washington by September 2—a day eagerly awaited by the crew at the Observatory. "Snow dances" under the full moon are not unheard of, though their actual effect on the weather is doubtful. Perhaps all that perspiration adds just enough moisture to the air to create snow. Whatever the reason, the Observatory crew welcomes snow; they have been deprived of the joy of sledding down the mountain for far too long.

Technically, early September is still summer—that is, everywhere but Mount Washington. Down in Boston, for example, the Red Sox are still wearing short-sleeved shirts as they dash their fans' hopes in yet another doomed-from-the-start pennant race. Meanwhile, on Mount Washington, winter weather hits a home run. Typically, two inches of snow fall in September, with twelve more in October. But you can't rely on averages, not where the weather is concerned; in October 1969, more than thirty-four inches of snow fell on Mount Washington.

The return of severe weather opens the door (sometimes literally) to a variety of icing-research opportunities. The Observatory is proud of its ongoing tradition of scientific study. An experiment nicknamed Cosmo counts incoming particles from the sun as they strike the earth. The goal of this thirty-year-old project is to see whether solar activity truly does have an effect on our global weather patterns.

The Observatory summit facility also houses experiments and research projects by the University of New Hampshire, the Federal Aeronautics Administration, the U.S. Army's Cold Regions Research and Engineering Laboratory, and the Appalachian Mountain Club.

Ever the observant scientists, the staff at the Mount Washington Observatory have concluded that fruits and vegetables can change the weather. "Bananas cause fog" is an accepted truth on the Rockpile. The evidence? As soon as banana bread comes out of the oven, clouds wash over the mountain, drowning the peak in fog. "And if someone eats the last banana on a foggy day, the mist immediately fades away and the sun comes back," explains crew member Lynne Host. At least, that is the theory. Further research is required to pin down the exact details of this phenomenon.

WINTER

"Well, if I've got to be stuck someplace working on Christmas, I guess this is the place to be," announces an Observatory staffer one snowy December day. She stands at the edge of the Observatory tower and whirls a psychrometer in the crystal-blue air.

Every six hours a crew member collects the precipitation can.

A thousand feet below the summit of Mount Washington, waves of misty cumulus clouds gush up the slopes and wash the boulders with a river of fog. High, above the summit the sky is still clear; a single wispy cirrus cloud dangles like a white string off the bottom of the sun. Off to the north, a small mountain stands wrapped in a white cocoon of snow; ice crystals sparkle and glitter on the peak. The sky is a cold blue dome.

Daylight never lasts long in winter. Early in the evening, the setting sun tumbles and rolls across the western horizon. As it sinks out of sight, colorful spears of light shoot up into the sky and the snowcapped mountains blush red. Slowly, night settles like a blanket over New England.

The winter solstice—also known as the festival of lights—occurs on December 21, the longest night of the year. It is when winter officially begins. Once the solstice passes, the days start to lengthen and the nights shrink—but the bitter cold of winter still lingers.

Cold and dark though it may be, the sky rarely fails to put on a show on Christmas Eve. Outside the Observatory, wind funnels the crisp air into an icy chisel, chipping away at the rime on the edge of the windows. Streams of gray fog pour out of the sky and cascade down the slopes of Mount Washington. Overhead, starlight and moonbeams wink on and off through the clouds. Below the summit, an undercast of low stratocumulus clouds surges against the hills of New Hampshire. A few high peaks poke up through this white ocean like islands afloat in the sky.

An Observer whirls a psychrometer to calculate dew point and relative humidity.

No one escapes a hard day's work on the Rockpile just because the calendar says it's a holiday. Weather never stops; it is the power of our atmosphere in action. Meteorologists at the Mount Washington Observatory spend the winter holidays on the summit, thrust into the quiet above the clouds, with plenty of time to contemplate the elements.

It's a long hike down to timberline (and an even longer hike back up) to get a Christmas tree to decorate, but the crew makes do. Here's a look

What is windchill?

Wind makes the air feel colder than it truly is. Even a soft breeze against your skin can make you feel as if you have suddenly stepped from a refrigerator into a freezer. Fortunately, the effect only applies to exposed skin, which is why ears, noses, and hands are so vulnerable to frostbite. Exposed skin will freeze solid in a fraction of a second when the windchill is below $-100°F$, as it often is on Mount Washington. For this reason, staffers on Mount Washington protect themselves with gloves, face masks, goggles, and balaclavas.

Remember, the windchill factor is only how cold it feels, not how cold it actually is. A typical windchill chart looks like this:

Wind speed (miles per hour)	Temperature (degrees Fahrenheit)							
	50	32	14	–4	–13	–22	–31	–40
10	41	18	–4	–26	–36	–49	–60	–71
20	32	7	–18	–44	–58	–71	–83	–96
30	28	1	–27	–54	–69	–81	–96	–108
40	27	–2	–31	–60	–74	–89	–103	–116
50	25	–4	–33	–62	–76	–90	–105	–119

Most windchill charts stop at forty or fifty miles per hour, adding the remark, "Wind speeds above forty miles per hour have little additional effect." Basically, once the wind speed plunges to the danger point, the numbers on the windchill chart don't matter much anymore. Cold is always cold, and deadly cold is always deadly. In either case, the end result is frostbite.

at Christmases past, from the pages of the Observatory logbook:

1995. *"Couldn't ask for a more perfect day than this. Nine degrees, sunny, ten-mph winds and undercast clouds. Almost caught up with summaries and paper-work left by the 'sick' crew. I must say those guys did make an effort at decorating."*

1991. *"A beautiful day on the Rockpile. Clear, cold, below zero all day. Windy at first, but calming down later. Dinner is turkey with all the fixings. Lots of calls from folks wishing us a Merry Christmas."*

1988. *"I hope the storm lets up enough to let Santa Claus through. On the night shift, I might even get to see him. Ever wonder if Santa has Doppler radar, or does he still rely on Rudolph?"*

1980. *"A cold night. Dinner was turkey à la frostbite, and no water to wash it down. Peak gust 135 mph."*

1977. *"Christmas on the Rocque Pyle. Al opens his present early (cheat, cheat). White Christmas with eight inches of new snow (the valley gets rain). Nice out now but getting cold fast."*

1978. *"Santa Claus ahead of schedule. Will stop at Mt. Washington for a snack before heading south. Majority of afternoon spent shoveling snow in the museum. It drifted in through a broken window."*

Winter is prime season for search-and-rescue operations. One evening, half an hour after the sun released one last warm ray of light, a frost-bitten camper crawled up to the summit in ninety-mile-per-hour winds. His face was pale white, like a ghost's, signaling the onset of frostbite. "My tent blew apart," he offered as an excuse, shivering with cold. Feeling pity, the summit crew took him in for the night.

The next day, an avalanche bulletin was faxed to the summit, warning of yet another risk to hikers and skiers in the White Mountains; "The John Sherburne Ski Trail is open to the bottom, but with a snow bridge cross-ing the river, so extra caution is advised. Holes in the snow have been known to appear and swallow the unwary."

Frostbite and avalanches are two dangers that await hikers and skiers who come to admire the stark beauty of the mountains in winter. But few people expect the snow to give way underfoot and swallow them up in an icy cocoon. Mount Washington isn't Everest, after all. On a pleasant winter day (if there ever truly is such a thing), the challenge of conquering Mount Washington's summit is relatively small; just park your car at the Pinkham Notch and scramble to the summit in a few hours. But remember: a day that starts with a warm smile from the sun can quickly and unexpectedly turn into a snarl of arctic air.

All in all, Mount Washington is a little mountain, dwarfed by the Himalayas and the Rockies. But climbing it still brings risks, especially in winter. Inexperience and reckless behavior, combined with relatively easy access to the high peaks, is often a deadly mix. Some hikers don't prepare for the possibility of sudden savage skies. More than 121 people have died on Mount Washington and in the nearby Presidential Range since British hiker Frederick Strickland succumbed to hypothermia in 1849.

When Mother Nature snarls and swallows the unwary, search-and-rescue teams—including staff from the Observatory, the State Park, the Appalachian Mountain Club, and the Forest Service—must find them and carry them to safety.

"The mountain claims another life today as a man is found expired on the Cog Railway track about 1½ miles from the base," reads one logbook

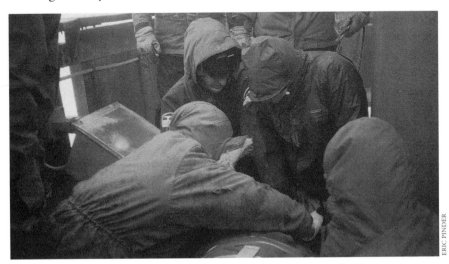

The crew participates in a search-and-rescue drill.

entry. "He was planning a day trip alone up to lakes [the Lakes of the Clouds] via the Ammonoosuc Trail. Did not come out on time so Fish & Game and the AMC with helicopter started the search. He had no ice ax, crampons or overnight gear with him."

Of course, some search-and-rescue operations have happy endings. "We monitored a so-called search and rescue one morning," recalls Observer Norm Michaels. "A couple was overdue at Lakes of the Clouds and were last seen in Edmunds Col, on the way over from Mount Madison. Eventually, the [AMC reservations] system figured out they had changed their reservations and decided to stay at Madison. They were 'found' in the bunkhouse."

Windchill and frostbite can combine to have a deadly effect. One icy January morning in 1994, the temperature dipped to –15°F, with winds gusting to sixty-five miles per hour, and according to the forecast, the weather would only get worse. An accident was just waiting to happen.

Ken Rancourt was driving the Observatory's Sno-Cat to the summit, leading a group of eight people on a winter EduTrip. (An EduTrip brings six or eight people to the top of the mountain, where they are introduced to topics such as geology, nature photography, or meteorology by members of the Observatory team.) The participants of that week's trip planned to stay overnight on the highest peak in New England and learn about the worst weather in the world. Little did they realize that they were going to learn more than they ever wanted to know.

They arrived safely on the summit even though winds kicked up blowing snow, creating whiteout conditions. Then the fun really began. Norm Michaels, shift leader that day, recalled the events in a short essay he wrote for the Observatory's *News Bulletin*:

> Just before dinner, the EduTrippers were ready to experience the high winds and take some photos outside. Several tried to cross the icy roof deck to the northwest railing. But none made it, since the strong gusty wind knocked them off their feet and slid them along until they reached a wind-sheltered spot from which they could crawl back to the door.

Around 7 p.m. we all sat down for a big turkey dinner. During the meal I took a phone call, a man who wanted to speak to Ken. I turned to the table, but Ken was gone.

"Amid the noise and jovial conversation of the dinner table," Ken told me later, "I basically heard a noise I didn't like. I thought at first it might be an antenna that had broken loose on the tower and was hanging by a cable, banging against the side of the building. Then I realized it wasn't rhythmic enough for that. I stood up and looked at Ralph and said I didn't like that sound. Let's go upstairs and check it out."

Outside, they found a half-frozen young man named Jeremy, banging on the door. They brought him inside and sat him down in the electronics room. He didn't have much strength left and he was complaining of the bright lights in the weather room hurting his eyes, which were almost frozen. He was not wearing goggles.

In the kitchen, we were still making merry around the dinner table when an urgent summons came from Ken on the intercom. Ken had called the hospital, and since it did not look like an evacuation would occur soon, we were advised to start warming [Jeremy's] hands.

The fingerless glove liners had to be cut off. His fingers were porcelain white. At first, we thought he had white gloves on.

Ken—"He was into hypothermia, exhausted and only semi-lucid, but was able to [tell] us over and over something he'd obviously recited to himself all the way over here, and that was the exact location of his friend. There was still another body out there somewhere. I called New Hampshire Fish & Game to alert them to the missing hiker."

Ralph—"We started treatment for hypothermia, the usual stuff—blood pressure checks, oxygen, warm sugary fluids. We moved some portable heaters in and wrapped him up. He was in wicked pain and shivered violently for a little while as his fingers defrosted and his temperature came back up. After a few more calls to the hospital, it was decided to switch to dry heat after the initial thaw."

Early Sunday morning we set a record daily minimum of –42°, and the winds never abated, averaging over seventy miles per hour all day. Ken made the decision that travel was simply too dangerous, so all our guests settled in for an extended stay. In the meantime, Androscoggin Valley Search and Rescue and Mountain Rescue Services made a monumental effort, attempting to rescue [Jeremy's] friend. Several suffered frostbite, and others called it the hardest rescue they had ever done. Sadly, their efforts were in vain. All they could do was recover the body.

We have learned that Jeremy has lost at least one fingertip. As one [EduTrip] visitor told us, "What you said about the weather was really true. This has been quite an experience."

Frostbite

Skin is mostly water, so it freezes and expands like ice. A severely frostbitten hand can swell to three times its normal size.

As skin cells start to freeze, the skin turns pale and numb. With superficial frostbite wounds, the skin is cold to the touch but still soft—it hasn't frozen solid. You won't notice any pain yet, but be careful. "You don't want to tug at your ear and have a chunk come off in your hand," says a grizzled, old-time search-and-rescue man.

Deep frostbite is also free of pain—until you try to rewarm the skin. Then, it turns into pure agony.

Safety tips. Bundle up at all times. Minor frostbite (when the skin is still soft, not frozen solid) can be treated by warming the frostbitten areas against warm skin. But severe frostbite is dangerous. The worst thing you can do is to refreeze already frostbitten skin. Do not thaw out a severe frostbite wound right away when there is danger of it refreezing—for example, if you are still in the wilderness. Wait until the danger passes, such as when you return to civilization and have easy access to a hospital.

The people who inhabit the cloudy world above tree line get frequent reminders of how hazardous conditions can be on the high summits. At times, the Mount Washington Auto Road disappears, erased by fog, and it is impossible to tell which way leads to solid ground and which way to a deadly fall, even when one is hiking on that fifteen-foot-wide "highway."

One winter morning during shift change at the Observatory, fog drowned the summit like murky ocean water. A meteorologist hoisted a pack on his shoulders and hiked down from the summit for his week off.

Meanwhile, a second crew member hiked up from below. They had coordinated their hikes and expected to meet each other halfway.

Coming up, one man noticed fresh footprints in the snow—footprints that led *down* the road. But no human was there. All the way up, he saw nothing but fog. When he arrived on the summit and pulled open the Observatory door, he was worried. "Where is he? I never saw him going down." Could he have fallen off the edge?

About the same time, the second man emerged from the fog near the base of the clouds and found fresh footprints—going up. Again, he saw no one.

In the most severe winter conditions, not one inch of skin can be exposed to the elements without risking frostbite.

Once he reached the base, he called the summit. "I saw footprints in places, but never passed anyone. Did he make it up OK?"

It turned out that the two men had passed each other along the road, perhaps just an arm's reach away. Because of the fog and wind they never saw or heard a thing.

"When you walk right by someone and never even notice, that's when you know the fog is thick," one of them remarked later.

It's a winter night, and a cold front is expected to pass through New Hampshire and Maine. On weather maps, a cold front is drawn, appropriately enough, as a spiky blue line, as if it were ready to stab the ground with its spears of cold wind.

Already the winds howls. When wind roars across the Observatory tower at 100 miles per hour, it's easy to imagine a great beast hunched outside the door, claws groping around the tower, trying to rip the basement out by the roots.

Downstairs in the Observatory, we hear wind hammering at the concrete walls. Each gust hisses through cracks in the window casings, spitting snow inside the building. Night Observer Lynne Host discovers a window slightly ajar, but to close it she must step over a mound of fresh snow. "Someone's going to have to shovel that up," she says, waving an arm at the snowdrift in the kitchen.

How often do you have to shovel up a snowdrift in your kitchen? Once or twice a year, if you are lucky enough to live on Mount Washington. Meteorologist Mark Ross-Parent recalls a time when he headed down to the valley for a week, closing his bunkroom door behind him. No one in the upcoming crew needed to use his room, so the door stayed closed—until one man thought he heard noises inside near the end of the week. He opened the door and found a room full of snow, a giant ice cube covering beds, dressers, and bunks.

"I remembered I had left the window open a crack, because it was warm," says Ross-Parent. "It took a long time to shovel out. I got a lot of grief for that."

Don't get the wrong impression; summit dwellers do enjoy their winters. Even with all the sledding, winter hiking, dessert-eating, snowshoeing, and snowball throwing, the Observatory crew also finds time to play. Other activities and hobbies besides observing weather include research on solar radiation, engineering, photography, and even stargazing.

We spend a lot of time looking at the sky, especially when there is a good likelihood of meteor showers. Meteors, or "shooting stars," are caused by chunks of asteroids that enter Earth's atmosphere. Friction with air molecules creates tremendous heat, which incinerates them in the upper atmosphere. Most people hear the word meteor and think of shooting stars. Seen from the ground, a meteor does look like a star streaking across the sky. Occasionally a bit of the rock survives its fiery plunge and lands on the Earth's surface as a meteorite.

Sawdust from the Logbook
Late 1995

"Halley's (rhymes with valley) Comet (rhymes with . . . you know) was spotted in 11-by-80 binoculars on a tripod. Only a faint coma was visible, as it is pointed straight at us at this time. It was very dim and at the limit of vision. Art said, 'Is that all there is?' Al could not see it at all, and Ken didn't even try to look."

When we are involved in meteorology at the Observatory, we are not studying burning asteroids, however; we are observing the weather. Why is the study of rain and clouds called meteorology? The term comes from an ancient book by Aristotle called *Meteorologica. Meteor* is Greek for "in the sky," and *ology* means "study of." Thus, meteorology is the "study of things in the sky."

In many ways, Aristotle was the world's first weatherman. But like every other weather observer in the world, he was known to blow a forecast or two. He also mixed up his facts. Aristotle believed that comets were atmospheric phenomena, just like clouds. Little did he know that they are actually distant, giant ice balls in orbit around the sun.

In the science of meteorology, a hydrometeor is made of water in the air, such as rain, snow, or hail. A lithometeor is made of solid dry particles, such as dust, smoke, or—in certain instances—volcanic ash. Haze is also a lithometeor; it is formed by tiny dry particles such as pollen or pollution, and casts a dark-bluish veil over the landscape.

In a sense, a "shooting star" is also a lithometeor. Although weather watchers on Mount Washington are more concerned with fog and haze than with asteroid debris or flying ice balls in outer space, we still take the time to admire shooting stars on cold, clear nights.

Once while I was working the night shift, the phone rang, a rattle of bells in the night. The caller told me to look up at the sky. I wrote down in the logbook what I saw that night: "Shooting stars galore. Someone calls up and asks if we saw a meteor with a green tail and a red nose. We were in the fog at the time, so we didn't see much of anything. Probably it was Rudolph making a test run."

Any crew member who manages to play the word cumulonimbus *during a Scrabble game wins by default.*

LIFE AT THE TOP

I step outside to take a weather observation, deep in the fog. The wind presses and prods my skin, stretched taut with cold across my cheekbones. Each gust slaps my face like the misty palm of a curious ghost who haunts the clouds, gently probing the outline of my skull. The hiss of wind is like the rustle of a million leaves.

The fog cascades across the mountain, a noisy river of moist air. Waves of mist ripple and churn at my feet. When I look east, turning my head into the breeze, the wind tugs at my ear, pulling me along the trail. I wrench my head back to one side, feel my ear settle back against my skull.

At a hundred miles per hour, clouds literally flow past the summit like a river; I sometimes think I could hop into a canoe and paddle away. I ponder how Henry David Thoreau described the lands in the clouds.

Thoreau climbed many mountains in New England and soon decided that mountains were "cloud factories." He climbed Mount Washington twice, in 1839 and 1858, but he never published a word about New England's highest peak. All that survives to document his two journeys are a few notes scribbled hastily in black ink in his journal.

When he approached the Mount Washington valley with his brother in 1839, he wrote, "Now we were in a country where inns begin—And we too now began to have our ins and outs." For days, Thoreau "shuddered through that Franconia where the thermometer is spliced for winter use, saw the blue earth heaved into mountain waves from Agiocochook." Later, he "heard the lambs bleat in Bartlett on the mountains late at night." Remarks about sheep appear quite often in his journal, but he says nothing about the jagged mica-schist boulders on Mount Washington or the windy world above tree line.

In 1846, Thoreau made a partial ascent of Katahdin, the tallest mountain in Maine. Like Mount Washington, Katahdin thrusts a wall of naked rock thousands of feet above timberline. Here Thoreau finally recorded his thoughts about the lands above the trees. His description could equally well describe the summit of Mount Washington: "I arrived upon a side-hill, or rather side-mountain, where rocks, gray silent rocks, were the flocks and herds that pastured, chewing a rocky cud at sunset. They looked at me with hard gray eyes, without a bleat or low. This brought me to the skirt of a cloud, and bounded my walk that night.

". . . Now and then some small bird of the sparrow family would flit away before me, unable to command its course, like a fragment of the gray rock blown off by the wind.

"I was deep within the hostile ranks of clouds. It was like sitting in a chimney and waiting for the smoke to blow away."

Thoreau fled back into the forest, where a sturdy roof of spruces held back the sky's wrath. In dying sunlight and by the red embers of his camp-fire, he wrapped himself in a blanket and scribbled fitfully in his journal. "It reminded me . . . of Atlas, Vulcan, the Cyclops, and Prometheus. Such was the Caucasus and the rock where Prometheus was bound. . . . It was vast, Titanic, and such as man never inhabits."

Recipes

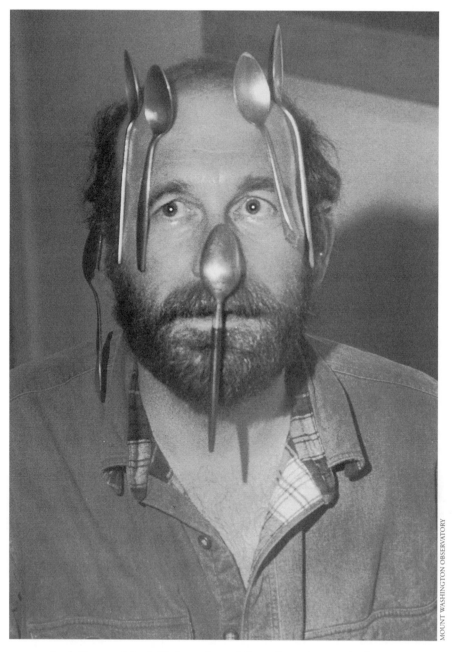

MOUNT WASHINGTON OBSERVATORY

Park Ranger Mark Holmes dressed for a formal summit dinner

Recipes from the Rockpile— Favorites from the Observatory Crew

If you have ever wondered what people eat on top of the windiest mountain in the world, you're not alone. Visitors to the summit are often shocked to learn that the Observatory boasts a full kitchen and a well-stocked larder.

"We thought you lived in tents!" said one astonished (but well-fed) visitor. He sat down on a couch in the Observatory's small living room and flipped through the pages of an old *National Geographic* magazine while the smell of fresh-baked bread wafted over the counter from the kitchen.

Life on Mount Washington offers all the comforts of home—until you step outside and get whisked off your feet by a hurricane-force breeze. But even when the temperature dips below –30°F, the wind shrieks like a banshee, and buckets of snow drop from the sky, the crew of the Mount Washington Observatory stay close to the stove and cook away their wintertime blues.

Ordering out for pizza is not an option when you are trapped on an icy mountaintop, but just because people live miles away from civilization doesn't mean they can't eat a civilized dinner—or two, if they get the chance.

This section features an assortment of recipes from the highest kitchen in New England. Some meals are old summit favorites, cooked often and eaten with relish. Others are family recipes contributed by Observatory members, volunteers, and staff. And still others I discovered written in sloppy handwriting on faded yellow pages in the "blue box" that sits on top of the Observatory refrigerator. The blue box has been around so long that its origins are forgotten, lost in the proverbial mists of time.

A recipe is only as good as the cook who makes it. Two people, starting with the same set of ingredients, can come up with entirely different results. Most Observatory meals are delicious and quickly devoured, but others end up as breakfast for the birds on Raven Rock.

To encourage cooking skills among the crew, the Observatory has a tradition of culinary awards. For example, the "Rookie Cookie Award" goes to the newcomer on the staff who makes a better-than-expected meal for the rest of the crew.

"I never won the Rookie Cookie Award my first year on the Rockpile," admits senior observer Norm Michaels. "Cooking was as much on-the-job training for me as were the daily weather observations. One night I made something sort of like a chili. Since my shift-mates liked spicy food, I added a lot of pepper. To be color consistent, I chose red pepper. Sadly, at the time, I didn't know the difference in heat between red pepper and black pepper. The result was so hot I thought we would all die. I had to serve ice cream with the main dish, and we still burned out our insides."

Nowadays, not much has changed. (Well, perhaps Norm's cooking has improved a bit. As a recent entry in the logbook notes: "Chief Observer Norm becomes Chef Observer Norm as he cooks up tonight's dinner: *pizza de resistance!*") Without a doubt, the crew still likes spicy food, as a glance at some of these recipes reveals.

We also have seasonal favorites, which is perhaps only appropriate for people whose lives are so oriented to weather. For example, spring is the season to enjoy Spring Thaw Soup (page 88), Rime Lemon Soup (page 87), Cocoa Mudslide Cake (page 127), Orographic Omelets (page 76), and Alpine Salad (page 93).

Since snowflakes occasionally fall on Mount Washington in the middle of summer, a Christmas dinner on the Fourth of July is not entirely out of the question. Many of our summertime favorites are actually appropriate for any season: Gourmet Deep Dish Pizza (page 115), Pasta Primavera (page 118), Guadalajara Night Chili (page 107), Sopaipillas (page 136), Blueberry Streusel Cake (page 128), and Banana Bread (page 86).

Popular recipes for the fall season include Pumpkin Pie (page 124), Apple Cake (page 129), Cheese & Wheat Beer Bread (page 79), Meat Lasagna (page 110), and Eggplant Parmesan (page 122).

In winter the idea is to stay warm, and meals cooked on the mountaintop live up to that ambition. "Strange hamburger/pepper/cheese/onion glop for dinner tonight," notes the logbook in December 1988. Fortunately, aside from that infamous "glop," winter brings in such favorite dishes as Cabbage Noodle (page 121), Kerosene Rice & Beans (page 120), German Goulash Soup (page 90), and Sticky Buns (page 133).

A Note about "low-altitude directions." If you have ever seen a "high-altitude alternative recipe" on a box of brownies, you know that changes in elevation and air pressure can have an effect on cooking. Most readers of this book probably live close to sea level, thousands of feet below Mount Washington's summit. For your convenience, all recipes in this book are designed for "low-altitude" kitchens.

Why mention this? Simply because water boils at a lower temperature in higher elevations, and that affects the cooking time for certain recipes. On Mount Washington, water boils at 202°F, instead of the standard 212°.

Air pressure—the "weight" of the atmosphere—is much lower on the summit, at 6,288 feet, than at sea level. On the mountain, average atmos-

How Not to Make Coffee

A story by former observer Al Oxton documents a mountain morning tradition.

"We used to make our coffee in an old electric percolator coffeepot," reminisces Al. "One of those kinds that sit on 'keep warm' after they're done perking. Another observer, John Howe, liked his breakfast coffee thick and strong. So he would often set up the pot to perk as part of his going-to-bed ritual. The pot would sit there with its 'keep warm' light on until John got up at five in the morning."

One day during shift change, John had his usual cup and went down the mountain. But the other shift switched to tea for the week. "Big John's eight-cup perk pot got pushed aside and sat in the corner, still on 'keep-warm,' all week. When he returned the following Wednesday, he practically had to shake the coffee into his mug. But he smacked his lips and thanked us for being so thoughtful as to make the coffee 'just the way he liked it.' It was a while before I told him it was the same pot he'd made the week before."

pheric pressure is 23.66 inches, compared to about 29.92 along the coast of Maine. Air on Mount Washington is also 18 percent thinner than at sea level. The weight of all the billions of air molecules in the atmosphere—200 miles of air—press down on lower air molecules to keep them snug against the Earth's surface. That's why air gets thinner the higher you go.

Unfortunately, the subarctic soil also gets thinner. Blizzard-like conditions discourage frequent trips to the grocery store, and chilly winds pretty much wreak havoc on anyone's attempts at gardening. So fresh fruits and vegetables are a seldom-seen luxury. The observatory stocks its pantry with an abundance of canned and frozen items, and the recipes reflect this fact.

In valley kitchens, feel free to substitute fresh produce for any canned/frozen ingredients listed in the following recipes.

Appetizers, Snacks, Beverages, and Breakfast Treats

Peak-Performance Deviled Eggs *(Contributed by Ken Rancourt.)*

12 eggs
1 heaping tbsp Gulden's brown mustard
2 tbsp mayonnaise
5 oz prepared horseradish (drain and save juice)
2 to 3 tsp ground cayenne pepper (optional)
sugar (optional)
paprika

Hard-boil the eggs and let them cool. Peel them, cut them in half lengthwise, and remove yolks. Chop yolks and mix them with mustard, mayonnaise, and horseradish.

Next, cover the mixture with cayenne pepper until it is red all over (omit this step for milder eggs). Generally, use 2 to 3 teaspoons of cayenne pepper, to taste. (Expect an initial jolt from the horseradish, but the real goal is for a slow rise of the heat from the cayenne to develop at the rear of the palate, spreading forward on your tongue to the rest of your mouth.) If you use the correct mixture, the cayenne should not be bitter. A dash of sugar will reduce the bitter taste of too much cayenne.

Finally, stuff the eggs with the yolk/mustard/cayenne mixture. If the mixture is too dry, add a little horseradish juice. Sprinkle with paprika to color the tops.

Party Cheese Ball

2 eight-oz packages cream cheese
2 cups extra sharp cheddar cheese, shredded
1 tbsp pimiento
1 tbsp chopped onion
1 tbsp chopped green pepper
2 tsp Worcestershire sauce
1 tsp lemon juice
½ cup finely chopped nuts

First, shred the cheddar cheese. Chop up the onions and green peppers. Mix all ingredients and form into a ball. Roll ball in chopped nuts to coat. That's all. (From the Blue Box.)

Grilled-Cheese Delight

In brutally cold regions, such as Alaska, Antarctica, or Mount Washington, a diet of high-fat foods can be surprisingly healthy—these foods help keep you warm. After all, there is no point in worrying about cholesterol if you're already shivering with severe hypothermia.

Here's a hot and simple lunch that probably contains far too much cholesterol but is delicious anyway.

> 4 slices bread (I prefer rye)
> cheddar or Swiss cheese, sliced
> 1 tomato, sliced
> butter or margarine
> ground red pepper (optional)
> garlic powder

Lay out the bread slices and slather them with butter or margarine. Flip two of the slices and layer the unbuttered sides with cheese and slices of tomato. Sprinkle on a little hot red pepper, if you choose. Cover with the remaining two slices of bread, buttered-side out.

In a frying pan, melt more butter or margarine with a dash or two of garlic powder. Then cook the two sandwiches over medium heat, flipping the sandwiches periodically until the cheese melts and both sides are toasted evenly.

Sherry Mushroom Pie *(Contributed by Barbara Shor.)*

Serve this delicious pie hot from the oven. Cut in small slices for appetizers, since it is very rich and filling. It also makes a fine main dish on a cold winter's night. Serve with an onion soup, crisp green salad, and fruit and cheese for dessert.

> pastry for a 2-crust, 8-inch pie
> 3 medium onions, minced

1 stick butter
2 to 3 tbsp light oil
2 lbs mushrooms, cleaned and quartered
2 to 4 tbsp good cream sherry (Harvey's Bristol Cream works best)
3 tbsp flour
1 cup light cream
salt and pepper to taste
grating of nutmeg and a few flakes of mace

Prepare the pie crust (using your favorite recipe). For a tender crust, chill dough for at least 2 hours before rolling out.

In a heavy skillet, sauté onions in butter and oil until transparent. Add mushrooms and cook for 4 or 5 minutes, until they are softened enough to give up their juices. Add sherry, and reduce the liquid in the pan by half.

Add flour and mix with a wooden spoon. Lower heat to a bare simmer and gently whisk in the cream. Do not allow sauce to boil! Add salt, pepper, nutmeg, and mace to taste. (Go easy on the spices, so that the mushroom flavor emerges.) Keep the consistency halfway between soupy and thick. Allow to cool.

Pour mushroom mixture into unbaked pastry shell and cover with lattice strips (to allow the filling to breathe). Preheat oven to 350o. Bake for 20 minutes, or until pastry is browned.

Party Punch

3 cups strong tea
3 cups water
3 cups orange juice
3 cups sugar
1½ cups lemon juice
1½ quarts ginger ale
2 pints fresh strawberries (bagged, frozen ones will do in a pinch)
ice

Just slosh all the ingredients together and this party punch is ready to go. Depending on how much ice is added, this recipe will make 1½ to 2 gallons.

Rum Swizzle (From the Blue Box.)

2 oz dark rum
2 oz white rum
4 oz orange juice
4 oz pineapple juice
¼ oz grenadine
1 or 2 dashes of bitters
unsweetened juices to taste

To make, just mix ingredients together and enjoy.

Granola (Contributed by Meredith Piotrow.)

4 cups regular rolled oats (not quick oats)
1 cup wheat germ
½ cup vegetable oil
½ cup honey
1 tsp vanilla
½ cup grated coconut (optional)
1 cup sunflower seeds (optional)
1½ cups Soya flakes (optional)
raisins (optional)

Mix ingredients together in a large bowl. If using raisins, add them after baking. Spread on cookie sheets and bake at 250° to 300°, stirring regularly. When oats are brown and crispy, remove from oven and cool. Store cooled granola in plastic bags or containers with lids.

Orographic Omelet (Contributed by Meredith Piotrow.)

1½ tbsp butter
4 eggs
4 tbsp milk
paprika
oregano
basil
salt
½ cup grated cheese (any kind)
tomatoes, diced (optional)

onions, diced and sautéed (optional)
mushrooms, diced and sautéed (optional)
cooked sausage, ham, or bacon (optional)
(Note: total quantity of filling should be about ½ to ¾ cup)

Melt butter in frying pan at medium heat. Be sure to spread butter so that it covers the entire pan. In a bowl, mix together eggs, milk, and seasonings to taste. Pour mixture into pan. Run a spatula around the outer edge of the omelet to make sure it isn't sticking or burning.

When egg mixture becomes almost firm, add your choice of grated cheese. Precooked sausage, ham or bacon may also be added. Diced tomatoes and sautéed onions are also a nice touch.

When the mixture is entirely firm (not runny), flip half the omelet back onto itself to form a half-moon. Serve hot. Will feed two people.

Mount Clay Cakers (spiced pancakes)

(Contributed by Chris Uggerholt; originally published in The Breakfast Cookbook: Favorite Recipes from America's Bed & Breakfast Inns, *Winters Publishing, 1990.)*

1¼ cups flour
⅛ cup sugar
1 tsp baking powder
½ tsp baking soda
½ tsp cinnamon
¼ tsp nutmeg
¼ tsp salt
1 egg
1¼ cups buttermilk
2 tbsp oil
butter (whipped)
maple syrup (warmed)
sliced bananas

In a large mixing bowl, stir together dry ingredients. In a separate bowl, mix together egg, buttermilk, and oil. Add the liquid to the dry ingredients (push down to make a "well" in the flour mixture before pouring), and stir until blended.

Spoon ¼ cup of batter onto a hot griddle or skillet for each pancake. Flip pancake over once the edges become dry. Serve with sliced bananas, whipped butter, and warm maple syrup.

Breads, Rolls, and Muffins

Cheese & Wheat Beer Bread *(Contributed by Lynne Host.)*

1½ cups beer (a hearty German beer works best)
⅔ cup water
½ cup olive oil
1½ cups whole-wheat flour
4 to 5 cups white flour
½ cup sugar
½ cup oatmeal
1 tsp salt
2 packages yeast
1 egg
2 cups sharp cheddar cheese

Pour beer, water, and olive oil into a saucepan and heat until warm (about 120°F). Next, in a large bowl, combine the warm liquid with whole-wheat flour and one cup white flour, plus sugar, oats, salt, yeast, and egg. Beat for 2 minutes.

Next, stir in the remaining white flour by hand. On a well-floured surface, knead the dough until smooth and elastic. Place in a greased bowl and cover; let the dough rise until it doubles in size (1 to 1½ hours). While dough is rising, shred 2 cups of cheddar cheese and set aside.

Punch down the risen dough, and divide in half. Work one cup of shredded cheese into each half. Finally, shape into 2 loaves and put into well-greased 9-by-5-inch loaf pans. Cover and let rise again 40 to 60 minutes.

Heat oven to 350° and bake 40 to 50 minutes. Be sure to remove the bread from the pans immediately.

Fake Corn Bread *(Contributed by Meredith Piotrow.)*

½ cup vegetable oil
½ cup white sugar
1 egg
1 cup milk

2 cups flour
2 tsp baking powder
a pinch of salt

Corn doesn't grow very well on the rocky, windblown summit of
Mount Washington, and sometimes it's inconvenient to trudge 20 miles
through a blizzard to the nearest general store. So when the Observatory
crew runs low on supplies, we make due with "corn-free" cornbread.

First, preheat the oven to 425°. In a large bowl, mix vegetable oil and
white sugar. Then add the egg and milk and continue to stir. Gradually stir
in the dry ingredients: flour, baking powder, and salt. Stir until all ingredients are well blended, then place dough in a greased and floured 9-by-9-
inch pan, and bake for 20 to 30 minutes, until firm. Serve hot.

No-Slice Lemon Bread

(Adapted from a recipe originally published in Time for Bread *by Susan Cummings. An
excellent and innovative book of bread recipes, this volume quickly became a summit
favorite. For further information or to order a copy, contact Susan Cummings, 86 Sussex
Dr., Kalispell, MT 59901.)*

1 tbsp yeast
1¼ cups warm water
1 lemon
2 tbsp powdered buttermilk
1 tsp salt
2 tbsp sugar
2 tsp vegetable oil
1 tbsp poppy seeds
1 cup white flour
¾ cup whole-wheat flour
¼ cup wheat germ
extra white flour (1½ to 2 cups)

Dissolve yeast in warm water. Squeeze the juice from the lemon and
grate the peel. Then add powdered buttermilk (or regular powdered milk),
salt, sugar, oil, poppy seeds, 1 tsp lemon peel, and 2 tbsp juice to the yeast
mixture. Stir in 1 cup white flour, all the wheat flour, and wheat germ (if

wheat germ is not to your taste, substitute an additional ¼ cup whole-wheat flour). Beat well.

Next, add enough additional white flour (1½ to 2 cups) to be able to knead the dough. Knead for 10 minutes, or until dough is smooth and elastic. Place dough in a greased bowl, cover, and allow to rise until doubled in size (about 45 minutes).

Punch down dough, knead a few more times, and cut the dough into 12 equal pieces. Let the slices sit for a few minutes. Meanwhile, grease a 9-inch loaf pan. Flatten each piece of dough and brush melted butter on one side.

Line up the dough pieces on edge in the pan until all 12 pieces fit inside. Let rise for another 30 minutes, until doubled.

Bake at 375° for 30 minutes, or until crust is browned. The loaf should sound hollow when tapped.

To serve, just peel off sections of bread and enjoy!

To experiment, omit poppy seeds and substitute a lime for the lemon. Note: the "no-slice" technique works just as well with most other bread recipes and makes a nice novelty.

Monkeying-Around Bread *(Contributed by Meredith Piotrow.)*

If you prefer, you can use your own favorite biscuit recipe for the dough. Or, to make things easier, just use 3 or 4 rolls of pre-made biscuit dough from the grocery store.

DOUGH

> ½ cup butter or margarine
> 2 cups flour
> 3 tsp baking powder
> 1 tbsp white sugar
> a dash of salt
> ⅔ cup milk

Cut butter or margarine into the dry ingredients. Then add milk and stir until dough is formed. Roll the dough into small (1- to 1½-inch-diameter) balls.

ADDITIONAL INGREDIENTS
> ¾ cup white sugar
> 2 to 3 tsp cinnamon
> ½ cup butter
> 1 cup brown sugar

Mix together the white sugar and cinnamon. Then roll the dough balls in the cinnamon-sugar mixture. Pile the biscuit balls in a well-greased pan (a small pan works best; the bread tastes better when biscuits are heaped on top of each other).

Finally, make a syrup by heating the butter and brown sugar until the mixture is boiling. Pour the hot syrup over the dough balls in the pan.

Bake at 350° for 30 minutes, or until the biscuits are done. Serve hot.

Good and Good-for-You Bread (Contributed by Barbara Shor.)

> 2 packages dry yeast
> ¼ cup warm water
> 1 tsp honey
> 2 cups milk (or soy milk)
> ¼ cup honey
> 3 tbsp butter
> 1 tbsp salt
> 2 cups whole-wheat flour
> 1 cup unbleached white flour
> 1 cup wheat germ
> 1 cup unprocessed bran
> 1 cup raw oats
> 1 cup chopped nuts (walnuts, almonds, or sunflower seeds)
> 3 tbsp orange rind, grated
> 1 apple (peeled, cored, and sliced)

Proof the yeast in a large, warmed bowl, adding warm water and 1 tsp honey (or raw sugar). Stir well, cover, and set aside for a few minutes in a warm spot, until yeast mixture is bubbly.

Meanwhile, scald the milk, 1/4 cup honey, butter, and salt in a saucepan. Stir until all ingredients are dissolved and well mixed. Put the milk mixture in the refrigerator or other cool place for a few minutes, and allow it to cool until it is no warmer than 110°F.

In a large bowl, mix together all the flours, wheat germ, bran, oats and nuts, and orange rind. Set aside.

Combine the yeast and milk mixtures, and stir in the apple slices. Also stir in 2 or 3 cups of the flour mixture. Beat until dough is smooth, then stir in the remaining flour mixture a cup or two at a time. You will end up with a stiff dough.

Turn out on a lightly floured board and knead for 15 minutes, or until dough is elastic (it will rebound to pressure and form surface blisters). Note: This dough will stay sticky and may require 1 or 2 extra cups of white flour while kneading. Be sure to slam the dough hard on the board several times as soon as it starts to turn elastic—this action helps develop the gluten and also smoothes the surface, so that less "extra" flour is needed. Place dough in a large greased bowl and turn once to moisten the surface of the dough.

Cover with a clean tea towel, and set in a warm place to rise. First rising takes approximately 1½ hours. Once dough has risen, turn out on a lightly floured board and knead lightly a few strokes. Cut in half and form into 2 loaves. Place loaves in well-greased bread pans and lightly grease the surface of the bread. If you like, slash a design on the top with a sharp knife. Let rise a second time, 45 minutes to 1 hour.

Bake in a preheated 350° oven for 50 minutes or until loaves sound hollow when tapped.

Anadama Bread

3 cups milk
¾ cup yellow cornmeal
¾ cup molasses
2 tbsp butter
2 tsp salt
2 packages dry yeast
¾ cup warm water

8 cups flour, sifted
extra butter, melted (for tops of loaves)

In a saucepan, heat milk to scalding. Remove from heat and slowly add the cornmeal, stirring constantly. Continue to stir until mixture is thick and smooth. Then stir in molasses, butter, and salt. Place in a mixing bowl and set aside (allow to cool until lukewarm).

Meanwhile, dissolve yeast in warm water and add to cooled cornmeal mixture. Gradually add about 5 cups of flour and beat until very smooth. Stir in remaining flour to make a soft dough. Turn out on a well-floured board, cover with a clean tea towel, and let rest for 5 to 10 minutes.

Knead dough for 6 to 8 minutes, until smooth and elastic. Place in a large, buttered bowl and turn dough to coat all sides. Cover and set in a warm place to rise until doubled in size.

Punch down dough and divide into 2 equal portions. To shape the loaves, flatten one portion and form into a 15-by-18-inch rectangle. Then start to roll it up, beginning at the narrow end. At each turn, seal the end with your fingertips. Pinch dough at the ends of each loaf to seal. Place in a buttered loaf pan (seamed edge down). Brush tops of loaves with melted butter and place in a warm area to rise until doubled.

Preheat oven to 350°. Bake 50 to 60 minutes, or until loaf sounds hollow when tapped. Remove from pans and place on a wire rack. Allow to cool before slicing.

Dinner Rolls *(Contributed by Mark Ross-Parent.)*

2 tsp active dry yeast
white sugar (just a dash)
½ cup warm water
6 cups white flour
2 tsp salt
1 cup warm water
1 cup milk (skim or whole)
2 tbsp olive oil
4 tbsp white sugar
1 egg white
sesame seeds

Add yeast and a dash of white sugar to ½ cup warm water, and set aside for 5 minutes to proof the yeast. In the meantime, combine the flour with salt and also set aside.

Mix together water, milk, olive oil, and sugar in a large bowl. Then to this mixture add the yeast mixture and the flour. Mix well until you form a ball of dough. Turn it out on a floured board and knead for 8 to 10 minutes, adding only as much flour as necessary to keep the dough from sticking. Place dough in an oiled pan, cover, set in a warm place, and let rise for one hour or until doubled.

Again, turn out the risen dough on a floured board. Deflate with a rolling pin. Cut dough into 12 equal pieces and roll them into balls. Place the balls in greased muffin tins and let rise again for 40 minutes to one hour.

Preheat the oven to 350°. Combine one egg white with a dash of water, and paint mixture on the rolls just before baking. Sprinkle the tops with sesame seeds and bake for 30 minutes or until rolls are deep brown. Serve hot with butter.

Blueberry Muffins *(Contributed by Lynne Host.)*

For best results, hike down to the Alpine Garden, just above tree line, and pick a pailful of wild blueberries. Be sure to leave some for the bears.

> 2⅔ cups flour
> ¼ cup rolled oats (uncooked oatmeal)
> 2⅔ tsp baking powder
> ½ cup white sugar
> ½ cup brown sugar
> 1 beaten egg
> 1 cup milk
> 4 tbsp melted butter
> 2 cups blueberries

First, sift together flour, oatmeal, baking powder, and sugars in a large bowl.

Next, add the well-beaten egg, milk, and melted butter. Stir just long enough to blend wet and dry ingredients, then fold in the blueberries—the more the merrier!

Pour the batter into greased muffin tins and bake at 425° for 25 minutes. Makes approximately 12 muffins.

Banana Bread *(Contributed by Lynne Host.)*

    3½ cups flour
    4 tsp baking powder
    1 tsp baking soda
    1 tsp cinnamon
    2 cups ripe mashed bananas (approximately 4 to 6 bananas)
    1½ cups sugar
    2 eggs
    ½ cup melted butter
    ½ cup milk
    1 cup chopped walnuts
    12-oz package chocolate chips (optional)

Preheat oven to 350°. In a small bowl, mix the dry ingredients. Set aside.

In a larger bowl, combine mashed bananas with sugar, eggs, and melted butter. Beat until creamy. Then add the flour mixture and milk, and mix until well blended. Finally, stir in the walnuts and chocolate chips (if you are using them).

Pour batter into 2 well-greased and floured 9-by-5-inch loaf pans. Bake for approximately 60 minutes and remove bread from pans to cool.

Soups, Sauces, and Salads

Cheesy Vegetable Soup

3 tbsp butter
3 tbsp all-purpose flour
2 cans (14.5 oz each) chicken broth
2 cups broccoli, coarsely chopped
¾ cup carrots, chopped
½ cup celery, chopped
1 medium onion, chopped
1 garlic clove, chopped
¼ tsp dried thyme
1 egg
1 cup heavy cream
1½ cups extra sharp cheddar cheese, shredded

Melt butter in a heavy saucepan. Add flour. Cook and stir over low heat until thick and bubbly, then remove from heat. Gradually blend in the broth, stirring constantly. Then add the chopped vegetables and thyme. Return to heat and bring to a boil. Reduce heat and let simmer for 20 minutes.

In a small bowl, blend egg and cream, then add several tablespoons of the hot soup mix. Return all to the saucepan, stirring until slightly thickened. Simmer gently for 15 to 20 additional minutes, then stir in cheese and heat until melted.

Makes 8 to 10 servings.

Rime Lemon Soup

"This light, fluffy egg-lemon soup looks a little like the rime ice that covers everything on the summit," says Professor Jill Schoof, the Observatory's Chair of Science and Engineering.

7 cans (14.5 oz each) chicken stock (equals 12 cups)
2 cups white rice (not precooked variety)
salt to taste
8 eggs
1 lemon, sliced very thin
juice from 4 lemons

Heat the broth until it boils, then add the rice and salt. Cover and simmer for 25 minutes. Remove from heat.

While the rice cooks, squeeze the juice from 4 lemons and cut a fifth lemon into thin slices.

Separate egg whites from egg yolks and beat the whites until they are stiff. Then add yolks and beat well. Continue to beat eggs while slowly pouring in the lemon juice. Next, slowly add 1 cup of hot broth to the egg mixture. Be sure to beat continuously, or else it will curdle.

Finally, blend the egg mixture into the remaining chicken broth and rice. Ladle into bowls and float a lemon slice in each bowl for decoration.

Makes 12 servings.

Spring Thaw Soup (Contributed by Kathy Bojack.)

This delicious soup is completely free of animal products, unless you choose to top it off with a little Parmesan cheese. Fat content is practically zero. From chopping board to serving bowls, the soup takes approximately 1½ hours to prepare.

> 1 to 2 tbsp sesame oil
> 2 lbs yellow or white onions, sliced
> 1 bulb garlic (5 or more cloves)
> 2 cups fresh spinach
> 2 cups fresh parsley
> 1 lb carrots
> 2 lbs tomatoes
> generous sprinkle of cayenne pepper (optional)

To begin, shred the carrots, slice the onions, and chop all other vegetables. Sauté garlic and onions in sesame oil (do not burn!). Add about a cup of water, and allow garlic and onions to simmer for a few minutes.

Add the rest of the vegetables, along with enough water to cover and establish a soupy texture. Cover and bring to a boil. Then reduce heat and simmer until the broth is rich and green.

If you like a little spice to your soup, sprinkle cayenne pepper in the broth. The cayenne will blend nicely if added early. Also add a dash of salt, if you like. Serving with some crusty bread that can be dipped into the soup is also a nice touch.

As is the case with many soups, this one tastes even better on the second day!

Squacolli Soup   *(Contributed by Dave Thurlow.)*

    1 butternut squash, 2 to 3 lbs
    1 large head broccoli
    2 cans evaporated milk (12 oz each)
    2 to 3 bouillon cubes (or miso to taste)
    1 stick butter
    1 lb sharp cheddar cheese (grated)
    lots of garlic and black pepper

Peel, chop, and boil the squash until soft. Be sure to save the cooking water. Chop the broccoli and steam it for just a minute or two. Melt butter and cheese in milk with the bouillon cubes or miso. Run it all through a blender, adding squash cooking water to attain the desired thickness. Serve with homemade bread.

Curried Butternut Squash Soup   *(Contributed by Jill Schoof.)*

    5 cups onions, finely chopped
    1½ sticks (¾ cup) unsalted butter
    4 or 5 tbsp fresh curry powder
    4 cans (14.5 oz each) chicken stock (equals 7 cups)
    7 lbs butternut squash, peeled and chopped
    5 McIntosh apples, peeled, cored, and chopped
    2 cups apple cider
    salt and pepper to taste
    2 Granny Smith apples, unpeeled and shredded, for garnish

In a deep pan, sauté the onions with the butter and curry over low heat until the onions are tender. Then add the chicken stock, the squash, and the McIntosh apples. Cover the pan and let simmer until the squash and apples are tender.

Pour the soup through a strainer and save the liquids. Add 1 cup of the strained liquid to the solids, then purée in a blender. Return to the pot.

Add apple cider and several cups of the leftover liquid (usually about 5 cups will do) until it is as thick as you want it. Add salt and pepper. Heat slowly until soup simmers. Serve with the shredded green apples sprinkled on top. Makes 12 servings.

German Goulash Soup *(Contributed by Lynne Host.)*

    2 lbs beef stew meat
    ¼ cup flour
    1 tsp black pepper
    6 strips bacon
    1 green pepper, chopped
    2 large onions, chopped
    1 garlic clove, diced medium
    2 tbsp paprika
    pepper to taste
    1 can (14 oz) stewed tomatoes
    3 cups beef broth
    2 large potatoes, medium diced
    ½ cup sour cream

First, cut the beef into ½-inch cubes, and coat with a mixture of ¼ cup flour and 1 tsp black pepper.

In a large cast-iron kettle, cook bacon until almost crisp. Add green pepper, onion, and garlic, and cook until tender. Then add the beef cubes, and cook until brown on all sides.

Sprinkle with paprika and pepper, and add tomatoes and beef broth. Cover and let simmer for 1½ hours or until beef is tender. About half an hour before serving, dice and add the spuds. Garnish each serving with a dollop of sour cream. Makes 8 servings.

Krummholz Mushroom Soup *(Contributed by Jill Schoof.)*

3 lbs mushrooms, finely chopped
2 bunches green onions, finely chopped
4 tbsp unsalted butter
salt and pepper
4 cans (14.5 oz each) chicken broth
2 cups water
1 cup dry white wine
2 cups whipping cream
4 egg yolks

Sauté the mushrooms and onions in the butter until tender, then add salt and pepper. Next, stir in the chicken broth, water, and wine. Cover and let simmer for 90 minutes.

In a separate bowl, combine the cream and the egg yolks. Add a little of the hot soup to the cream and eggs, stirring constantly. Then stir the heated cream mixture back into the soup pot, and heat to serving temperature. Be careful not to let it boil, or the soup will curdle.

Peanut Butter Soup

Former observer Al Oxton, now working in Antarctica, created (and continuously experimented with) this old summit favorite. Generally, this is a rich, creamy soup. About a cup is enough to start dinner.

1 medium onion, diced
2 to 3 cloves garlic
¾ cup peanut butter
¼ cup butter
¼ cup flour
milk
water
a dash of black pepper
whole peanuts for garnish

Start with a 10-inch cast iron skillet. "None of those fancy high-tech flimsy things, nor aluminum either," says Al. "The skillet must have a tight-fitting cover too. And use wooden spoons for stirring."

Sauté the chopped onion and garlic in olive oil. After 1 or 2 minutes, add peanut butter—crunchy works best—and regular butter. ("That's real butter," insists Al. "I will not be responsible if you use any of those sickly spreads.")

Now, lower the heat and cook until all the butter and peanut butter melt and blend. Then add flour. The flour is important because it binds the fats with the yet-to-come-liquids.

When the flour is all taken up by the fat, add milk. Use as much milk as necessary to adjust thickness to taste. Stir very slowly, and add milk a bit at a time. "You can also add water or chicken broth to blend the flavor one way or the other," adds Al.

"It is important to keep the whole mess moving while it is thick, so as not to scorch it. Nothing is worse than burnt peanut butter soup." Once you have adjusted the thickness to suit your taste, sprinkle on a little black pepper. Let the soup simmer for 10 minutes more, stirring occasionally.

Serve in warm bowls, and garnish with 3 roasted peanuts (still in their shells) floating on top. Crackers and a thick grape preserve work well on the side.

Creamy Garlic Sauce for Pasta

2 tbsp (or more) minced garlic
1 onion, minced
fresh ground pepper to taste
2 tbsp butter
1 cup light cream (use milk for a thinner sauce)
¾ cup grated Parmesan cheese
½ cup butter

Sauté garlic, onion, and pepper in 2 tbsp butter. Then add cream, Parmesan cheese, and rest of butter. Stir all together until sauce is smooth and hot. Pour over hot pasta.

Quick Vegetable Tomato Sauce

How many vegetables you use in this quick pasta sauce depends on how much you plan to eat for dinner. Add enough chopped and diced veggies so that noticeable chunks appear in the sauce.

broccoli, chopped
green pepper, chopped
onions, diced
2 garlic cloves, diced
mushrooms, sliced
1 tbsp olive oil
½ to 1 cup tomato sauce
basil
fresh ground pepper
Parmesan cheese
dollop of sour cream (optional)

Sauté vegetables and mushrooms in olive oil. Then stir in tomato sauce (add extra if you have a crowd for dinner). Add basil and pepper to taste. Pour over hot pasta and top with Parmesan cheese and sour cream.

Alpine Salad

1 head leaf lettuce
½ head iceberg lettuce
2 to 3 tomatoes, chopped
1 cucumber, sliced
1 onion (or more), sliced and diced
2 to 3 radishes, sliced up nicely
2 carrots, thinly sliced
1 pepper, medium diced
1 can (14 oz) black olives, drained
½ jar (14 oz) pepperoncini, drained
2 small cans mandarin oranges, drained
2 tsp dill weed

Arrange ingredients neatly in a wooden salad bowl. Add black olives and pepperoncini and mandarin oranges. Mix it all up. Finally, sprinkle the top with the secret ingredient: dill weed.

Serve with a fine choice of salad dressings, and chomp down.

Orange-Cranberry Delight (Contributed by Sarah Shor.)

This colorful treat should be prepared at least 4 to 6 hours ahead.

CRANBERRY GELATIN

>   1 package plain gelatin
>   ½ cup boiling water
>   ¾ cup cranberry juice
>   ¾ cup orange juice

Soften the gelatin in boiling water, then stir and mash it with a fork until it is completely dissolved. You may have to squeeze the gelatin through a small sieve to get all the lumps out.

Combine cranberry and orange juices in a large refrigerator container, stir in the dissolved gelatin, and chill in a refrigerator until partially set (about 1 to 1½ hours).

CRANBERRY RELISH

>   12-oz package whole cranberries
>   ¼ to ½ cup sugar
>   1 tbsp grated orange peel
>   1 tbsp orange liqueur (Grand Marnier)
>   1 orange, peeled and sliced in rounds

First, wash the cranberries in a colander and make sure all stems have been removed. Chop the cranberries coarsely in a food processor, then pour them into a heavy pot and stir in sugar. Cook for 3 to 5 minutes until slightly softened. (At this stage, taste to see if more sugar is needed.)

Bring the mixture to a high simmer, then remove from heat and stir in the orange peel and orange liqueur. Chill in the refrigerator until partially set.

Now it is time to combine the two parts of this dessert, both of which have been cooling in the refrigerator. When the gelatin mixture has started to solidify, very gently stir it into the chilled pot of cranberry relish.

For decoration, line the bottom of a chilled gelatin mold with orange slices, then pour in the gelatin-relish mixture. Be sure to keep it below the rim of the mold. Let the mixture sit in refrigerator for at least 4 to 6 hours, preferably overnight.

When you are ready to unmold, have a large serving tray or a flat platter ready (Either chill the platter or run it under cold water and dry it before use.) Next, dip the mold (with the orange-cranberry mixture) into a bath of hot water. Be careful to keep the rim above the water. Gently jiggle the mold from side to side in the hot water until the relish moves freely.

Put the serving platter upside-down over the top of the gelatin mold and turn the whole thing over in one smooth motion. Gently remove the mold, and enjoy.

Main Dishes

Tip-Top Tuna *(From the Blue Box.)*

Tip Top House, built in 1853 and gutted by fire in 1914, once offered visitors sanctuary from the winds and, sometimes, a bite to eat, as well. The stone-walled building that stands today is a historical re-creation, owned by the state of New Hampshire. Travelers to the summit in the 1800s might have indulged in meals like this one—not fancy, just filling.

    1 lb (uncooked) noodles or macaroni
    2 tbsp margarine
    1 can peas (or 1 ten-oz pkg frozen peas, cooked)
    2 cans condensed cream of celery soup
    2 cans tuna (7½ oz each)

Boil noodles, then drain them and add margarine, tossing noodles to coat them. Meanwhile, drain the peas and add to the undiluted soup. Heat to a simmer. Drain tuna and spread over warm noodles. Pour soup over tuna. Heat over low heat (in the old days at Tip-Top House, they used to heat over a low fire), stirring occasionally, for 2 to 3 minutes.

Chicken with Onions and Potatoes

    2 tbsp butter
    2 tbsp olive oil
    2 cloves garlic, minced
    1½ tsp Italian seasoning
    hot-pepper sauce to taste
    4 whole chicken breasts, split
    4 medium onions, quartered
    4 potatoes, cut into about 1-inch chunks

In a large roasting pan, place butter, olive oil, garlic, seasoning, and as much hot pepper sauce as you like, but don't mix them yet. First, set the oven to 400° and while it's warming up, place the pan inside until the butter melts.

Once the butter is melted, stir to mix it with the other ingredients. Then place chicken pieces in the pan, turning them until they are coated with the butter mixture. Place the chicken skin-side up in the center of the pan.

Arrange onions and potatoes (cut-side up) all around the chicken. Brush each piece with the butter mixture. Bake for about 50 minutes, until the chicken is tender.

Chicken Paprikash (Contributed by Danny Johnson.)

"To enhance the appreciation of this Eastern European favorite," advises Park Ranger Danny Johnson, "whip it up after a drive through Pinkham Notch, all the while imagining you're actually on a blood-curdling journey through the Carpathian mountains, racing against the sunset. Be sure to leave the skin on the chicken so the bright orange sour-cream gravy will be swirled through with the lovely, dark red grease. You can worry about your arteries later."

> vegetable oil
> butter
> 3 to 4 lbs chicken (in pieces)
> 5 large onions, chopped
> 4 or more tbsp Hungarian hot paprika
> salt and pepper to taste
> 12-oz can peeled tomatoes (equals 1 pound)
> 3 cups chicken broth
> 3 to 4 tbsp flour
> 2 tbsp sweet paprika (or hot, if preferred)
> 12 oz sour cream

In a large pot, cauldron, or Dutch oven, brown the chicken pieces in oil and butter. Remove from pot and set aside. In the same pot, sauté onions and hot paprika until onions turn glossy red. Return chicken to pot.

Season liberally with salt and pepper. Add tomatoes and broth (enough to cover chicken). Bring to a boil. Cover, reduce heat, and simmer 1 hour, or until chicken is tender.

In a separate bowl, stir flour and sweet (or hot) paprika into the sour cream. Remove chicken to serving dish. Add some of the liquid in the pot to the sour cream mixture, then whisk this into the pot. Bring just barely to a boil, stirring. Pour over chicken and serve with egg noodles.

Chicken Cacciatore *(Contributed by Danny Johnson.)*

"Skillet size is important for this recipe. Be sure to use an iron skillet big enough for an elephant to sit in and heavy enough to serve as weaponry," says Danny Johnson. "Utilizing it in either or both these manners just before confecting this crowd-pleaser adds greatly to the old-world charm of this rich meal."

¼ cup olive oil
4 lbs chicken, in pieces
4 cloves garlic, minced
1 or 2 large onions, in fat slices
1 large green pepper, in wide strips
2 tbsp salt
1 tsp white pepper
cayenne pepper (several dashes)
¼ tsp rosemary
2 bay leaves
½ tsp thyme
1 tsp basil
¼ tsp marjoram
½ cup Chianti or dry white wine
1 can (28 oz) Italian peeled tomatoes
1 can (15 oz) tomato sauce
1 can (6 oz) tomato paste
2 tbsp brandy
1 cup sliced mushrooms

In a large, deep skillet, brown chicken pieces in olive oil. Then remove chicken and set aside. Add and sauté: garlic, onion, and green pepper, then return chicken to pan. Sprinkle seasonings and herbs over all. Mix together wine, tomatoes, sauce, and paste and pour over chicken pieces. Sprinkle brandy over all.

Cover and simmer one hour or until chicken is tender. Stir occasionally to prevent scorching. Add mushrooms for last 10 minutes of cooking time. Serve over pasta.

Chicken and Ham Rolls *(Contributed by Lynne Host)*

4 whole chicken breasts (boneless and skinless)
½ cup sharp cheddar cheese, grated
¾ cup cooked ham, diced medium
6 tbsp olive oil
½ cup dry white wine

Pound the chicken breasts as thin and flat as possible. Top each one with equal portions of cheese and ham. Then roll it up and tie with butcher's string to form a bundle.

In a frying pan, sauté chicken pieces in olive oil until brown (usually no more than 6 minutes). Add wine, cover, and cook another 6 to 10 minutes or until tender (*not* dry).

Serves 4 normal people or one hungry mountain meteorologist.

Chicken Crunch *(From the Blue Box.)*

½ cup chicken broth (or milk)
3 cups cooked chicken, cubed
¼ cup onion, finely chopped
⅓ cup almonds, slivered
2 cans condensed cream-of-mushroom soup
1 cup celery, diced
1 small can water chestnuts, drained and sliced thin
3-oz can chow mein noodles

Blend all ingredients and pour into greased casserole. Bake 40 minutes at 350º. Serves four big eaters.

Emil's Chicken Medallions *(Contributed by Guy Gosselin.)*

Served cold, this dish is great picnic fare, but hot out of the oven, it makes a gourmet delight! Chicken Medallions made their debut during the thirtieth anniversary Mount Madison Volunteer Ski Patrol picnic in June 1996.

6 boneless chicken-breast halves
2 tbsp minced onion
2 tbsp minced sweet red pepper

2 tbsp minced celery
1 package cream cheese (at room temperature)
¼ cup butter or margarine
2 tbsp flour
3 cups milk
2 envelopes powdered chicken bouillon (or two cubes)
1 clove garlic, minced
juice from a ¾-inch lemon wedge
1 tsp grated lemon rind
salt and pepper to taste
dried cilantro

ALSO

pastry for a large, double-crusted pie
about 25 toothpicks (if you use them carefully)

Pound the chicken breasts flat using a regular hammer and a small, smooth piece of plywood or board. Set aside. Sauté the minced onion, sweet red pepper, and celery in some butter, then combine with the softened cream cheese to make filling. Spread half the filling mixture over flattened chicken breasts, and roll up the breasts. Secure with toothpicks, making sure to seal the ends as best you can.

Arrange the rolled breasts on a collapsible vegetable steamer (or similar device) and lower into a covered kettle or wok to parboil (about 15 to 20 minutes). Check from time to time to make sure the filling is not leaking out. Meanwhile, roll out the pie dough.

When the chicken is firm, remove toothpicks. Cut rectangular sections of pie dough large enough to cover each rolled breast. Divide the remaining filling into 6 portions, spreading one portion on each of the pastry pieces. Plunk the rolled breasts down on the filling and bring the edges of the pastry dough together along the top of the breast, letting the dough overlap by about ¼ inch. Use toothpicks to secure the roll across the top. (What? You threw away the toothpicks! Well, you will need to get some more.) Leave about an inch of dough at each end of the roll. Fold and tuck the flaps for maximum closure, and secure them with toothpicks as well.

Place rolls in a rectangular baking pan and bake at 350° until pastry is slightly browned, approximately 30 minutes. Refrigerate the cooked rolls.

Make the sauce by melting the ¼ cup butter (or margarine) in a saucepan. Then, with the saucepan off the fire, mix in the flour. The flour will start to thicken in the hot butter, so make sure you cream it as much as possible. Adding a little bit of milk will stop the thickening process and make a nice, creamy mixture.

Gradually add the rest of the milk and cook over medium heat, stirring constantly, until thickened. Now add the powdered bouillon and minced garlic, cooking for several more minutes over low heat. Remove from stove and add the lemon juice and grated lemon rind, stirring to blend. Add salt and pepper to taste, but watch the salt (there may already be enough in the bouillon). A couple shakes of cilantro will make a tasty garnish.

When the chicken rolls are well chilled, remove the toothpicks (you can throw them away now!) and slice each roll crosswise into ¼-inch medallions with a sharp knife. Lay out the medallions by overlapping them on a platter in 2 or 3 rows. Top with the sauce and serve either hot (by microwaving for 4 to 5 minutes) or cold.

Serves 6 to 8 people.

Peabody Baked Beans *(From the Blue Box.)*

> 2 cups beans
> ¼ lb salt pork, sliced about ¼-inch thick
> 1 large onion, sliced
> 3 tbsp brown sugar
> 3 tbsp molasses
> 1 tsp salt
> ½ tsp dry mustard
> 2 tbsp catsup

Here is a simple recipe that takes two days to make.

First, soak the beans overnight: that takes care of Day #1. On Day #2, sear the pork and sauté the sliced onion. Combine all ingredients in a pressure cooker. Use the water from the soaked beans to cover.

Pressure-cook for one hour, letting the pressure drop of its own accord for 15 minutes more. Serve with pride.

Seafood Casserole

> 1 large onion, chopped
> 1 green pepper, chopped
> 2 celery stalks, chopped
> 2 tbsp butter or margarine
> 10-oz can condensed cream of mushroom soup
> 10-oz can condensed cream of shrimp soup
> 10-oz can condensed cheddar cheese soup
> ½ cup milk (use more if necessary)
> 2 nine-oz cans shrimp
> 1 nine-oz can crab or lobster
> 4 cups cooked rice
> salt to taste
> bread crumbs
> Parmesan cheese

Sauté onion, pepper, and celery until tender in butter or margarine. Add soups, milk, and seafood. Stir in rice and salt. Place it all in a 2-quart casserole dish and cover with crumbs and cheese. Bake at 375° for 30 to 45 minutes.

Makes 6 to 8 servings.

Crabmeat Foo Yung *(From the Blue Box.)*

I suppose the observatory crew could hunt for crabs and lobster down at Lakes of the Clouds. But somehow it seems easier to buy packaged crab-meat at the store. Here is a good crabmeat recipe.

> 1 cup (8 oz) crabmeat
> 1 cup bean sprouts
> ½ cup onion, julienned
> ½ cup celery (finely sliced)
> 3 tbsp cooking oil
> 6 eggs

1 tbsp soy sauce
1 tbsp cornstarch
1 tsp salt
a dash of pepper

Put crab and bean sprouts in a large bowl and set aside. Sauté onion and celery in oil for about 5 minutes, until vegetables are limp. Then add to crab.

In a separate bowl, beat eggs. Then add soy sauce, cornstarch, and salt and pepper to taste. Pour over crabmeat and mix well. Drop tablespoons of the mixture in a greased skillet and cook over medium heat, turning once, until brown on both sides. Repeat this step until all of the mixture is browned. Keep the crab cakes warm while making the sauce.

SAUCE

½ cup water
2 tsp sherry
1 tbsp soy sauce
2 tsp cornstarch

Mix ingredients and cook over medium heat, stirring constantly, until thick. Then pour sauce over warm crab cakes and enjoy.

Shrimp Mold (From the Blue Box.)

Be sure to make this mold the day before you expect to eat it.

8-oz package cream cheese
1½ cups mayonnaise
1 can tomato soup (undiluted)
2 packages unflavored gelatin
¼ cup cold water
1 cup celery (finely chopped)
¼ cup finely chopped onion
¼ tsp garlic powder
10-oz can shrimp

Beat cream cheese and mayonnaise until smooth and set aside. Heat soup to lukewarm. Thoroughly mix cold water with gelatin then add the gelatin mixture to warm soup. Add soup mix to mayonnaise mix and combine with other ingredients. Blend well and pour it all into a large ring mold. Refrigerate overnight.

Salmon Loaf *(Contributed by Jane Pinder.)*

> 1 no. 1 can salmon (about 2 cups)
> ⅓ cup milk
> ⅔ cup bread crumbs
> 2 eggs
> 1 tsp salt
> 1 tbsp lemon juice
> 1 tbsp parsley flakes
> cayenne to taste

First, drain the oil from the can and flake the fish. Soften bread crumbs in milk for 5 minutes. Stir in unbeaten eggs, salt, lemon juice, parsley, and cayenne. Then stir in fish and pour mixture into a greased loaf pan. Set loaf pan in a larger pan of hot water and bake at 350° for 1 hour.

Aroostook Potato Scallop with Pork Chops *(Contributed by Jane Pinder.)*

> 8 cups potatoes, peeled and thinly sliced
> 2 medium onions, thinly sliced
> 1 tsp salt
> ½ tsp pepper
> 1 quart milk
> 6 to 8 center-cut pork chops

Place potatoes in a large casserole dish (or a large frying pan at least 2½ inches deep). Add onions, salt, pepper, and half of the milk.

Place pork chops on potatoes in a single layer. Then add the remaining milk. Cover with aluminum foil and cook 1 to 1½ hours at 400°. (Keep an eye on the dish, so that the milk does not boil over in the oven.) Turn pork chops over when partly done and baste with milk from the dish or pan, then continue cooking.

When done, this meals feeds 6 to 8 people. Spices or cheeses can be added to taste.

Canadian Spicy Pork Pie *(From the Blue Box.)*

    3 lbs lean pork, cubed
    2 large onions
    6 medium potatoes
    2 cups water
    2 tsp salt
    1½ tsp sage
    ½ tsp cinnamon
    ¼ tsp cloves
    pastry for 1 nine-inch double-crust pie

Combine pork, onions, and potatoes in salted water and bring to a boil. Let simmer for one hour and then pour off the liquid into a separate bowl (the resulting steam is an example of "hot fog"—water vapor condensing in the cooler air). Finally, pour 1 cup of the liquid plus sage, cinnamon, and cloves back onto the meat and mix well. Serve as is, or put into pie shell and bake at 350° for approximately half an hour.

Chinese Pork Chop Suey *(From the Blue Box.)*

    ¼ cup oil
    1 cup diced pork or beef
    1 cup onion, chopped
    1 cup celery, chopped
    1 can (14 oz) bean sprouts
    ½ cup hot water
    2 tsp cornstarch
    1 tsp sugar
    3 tsp soy sauce
    ½ cup cold water

Heat the oil in a frying pan, and sauté the meat with the onion and celery. Add the sprouts when the meat is almost browned. When the pork is cooked, pour hot water into pan and stir to blend.

Next, mix the cornstarch, sugar, soy sauce, and cold water. Add to the frying-pan mixture and stir. Let simmer for about 10 minutes more, stirring frequently.

Unnamed Dish (Contributed by Jane Pinder.)

> 2 tbsp oil
> 3- to 4-lb round roast, sliced ¼-inch to ½-inch (bottom or top round
>   roast works best)
> 16-oz can tomato sauce
> 2 large onions, thinly sliced
> salt and pepper to taste
> a dash of sea salt
> parsley flakes
> 4 fresh mushrooms (or 8-oz can of mushrooms)
> 2 tbsp butter

Spread oil in a heavy saucepan or a large Dutch oven, and make layers of steaks (from the sliced round roast), tomato sauce, onions, and seasonings. Repeat until all steaks are used. The top layer should be tomato sauce with seasonings. Cover and simmer for 2½ to 3 hours.

Just before serving, sauté mushrooms in butter. Pour over the cooked mixture when done. Makes 6 to 8 servings.

Leftover Casserole

This is a great way to clean out a crowded refrigerator and use up leftover rice. For a vegetarian dish, simply omit the meat.

> 2 to 4 cups cooked rice (1 cup uncooked rice)
> 2 tbsp margarine or butter
> 1 small onion, finely chopped
> salt and pepper to taste
> 2 to 3 dashes Worcestershire sauce
> 1½ cups cheddar cheese, grated
> 4-oz can sliced mushrooms (save the liquid)
> 1 cup milk
> 1½ cups diced leftover chicken, beef, or pork (or a combination)
> 1½ cups peas or green beans (or assorted vegetables)
> ¾ cup crushed crackers
> paprika to taste

(If you are not using leftover rice, first cook a fresh batch as directed on package.)

In a large cast-iron frying pan, place butter, onion, salt, pepper, Worcestershire sauce, 1 cup of the grated cheese, and the liquid from the canned mushrooms (if you are using fresh mushrooms, use liquid from the cooked or canned vegetables). Cook over low heat, stirring occasionally, until onion is tender and cheese is melted. Add all remaining ingredients (except paprika and cracker crumbs), placing the last ½ cup grated cheese on top.

Cover the pan loosely (leave a vent). Simmer 25 minutes. During the last 10 minutes, top with paprika and cracker crumbs. Serve directly from frying pan.

Guadalajara Night Chili *(Contributed by Guy Gosselin.)*

Caution: This chili is not for the faint-hearted (that goes for the cook as well as the diners). Hot foods such as chili have an interesting history. Believe it or not, there is a good rationale for making food so hot that you can't taste it; the use of searing chili peppers and spices is reputed to be no more than a strategy for making "spoiled" meat edible. For people who hate to waste food, this recipe is ideal.

The cook's first responsibility is to check the refrigerator and freezer for any leftover meat that would normally be passed over. If organ meat, pork, beef, game, or chicken linger in your icebox a little past their expiration date, consider them now. Be sure to cut off any mold or "bad" meat. A long simmer will destroy bacteria and transmogrify gaminess into delicate flavor. Of course, it's fine to use fresh meat, as well.

> 1 to 2 lbs dry pinto beans
> ¼ lb salt pork, cut in strips or cubes
> 1 or 2 bags (3 oz each) dry chili peppers (the hotter the better)
> 1 lime, peeled
> 1 cup chicken bouillon
> 1½ to 3 cups water
> 4 to 6 large cloves garlic
> fresh ground pepper
> celery salt
> cumin

4 tbsp lard or margarine for sautéing
3 to 6 medium onions, slivered
1 sweet red pepper, sliced into 2-inch strips
2 lbs hamburger
2 lbs stew beef (don't trim off the fat)
up to 2 lbs salvaged meat, trimmed (don't flinch)
2 to 4 cans (28 oz each) whole tomatoes with juice
3 celery stalks
2 lbs chorizo or other sausage
1 oz chili powder

Note: This dish requires that you start the day before!

Soak the beans overnight. When softened, boil them with salt pork strips until most of the fat is absorbed and beans are tender (this usually takes about 4 hours). Don't throw away the boiled-down liquor—you may want to use some later in the chili itself.

Also ahead of time, cut the stems and pull the loose veins out of the dried chili peppers. (Salvage the seeds and store them temporarily in a blender.) Soften the peppers in water for a couple of hours.

Make the chili sauce by combining the soaked peppers and pepper seeds in the blender with the peeled lime, chicken bouillon, water, and half of the garlic. Add fresh ground pepper, celery salt, and cumin to taste. Purée and set aside.

Sauté onions and sweet pepper in the bottom of a 5-gallon kettle with a bit of lard or margarine. Add hamburger, beef, and salvaged meat. Fry for a while with more pepper, salt, and the rest of the garlic (minced). If you are not using any salvaged meat, add extra hamburger and/or cubed stew beef and pray this turns out OK!

After the meat is fairly well cooked, throw in the canned whole tomatoes (juice and all) and whack away at the them with a sharp knife (this may make you feel better if you've had a hard day). Slice up the celery and throw it in. Cut the chorizo or other hot sausage into half-inch pieces and add them to the pot, as well.

Next, add the beans and salt pork strips, plus as much of the chili sauce as you think wise. A blender-full is about right, but do it a half-cup at a time and taste the results (you want the hot chili sauce to enhance the flavor, not mask it). You will want to add regular chili powder for body, but do it in increments and to taste. If the sauce still doesn't taste quite right, you have the liquor from the beans and pork to make adjustments. You can also add more garlic or salt and maybe some cilantro.

Let the chili simmer for at least 3 hours, stirring occasionally. Taste and make further adjustments as needed.

After all that work, this is the easiest step: Relax and have a beer or margarita. Invite your guests to taste and comment (they can also make suggestions, but don't pay any attention).

"By now, it is too late in the cooking process to make any fundamental changes," explains the creator of Guadalajara Night chili, Guy Gosselin. "If, by chance, you have messed up, just smack your lips and pretend it is the best recipe you ever made. Those who are suggestible will believe you, and will become valuable allies in convincing others. Mix more margaritas for those who persist in their disagreement, and they will eventually come around."

Serve with sopaipillas and warm honey. Sweet sopaipillas make a nice complement for the chili. The hotter the chili, the more welcome the sopaipillas.

Pepperoni Bake (Contributed by Jim Studley.)

      6 oz pepperoni, sliced thin
      ¾ cup flour
      1 egg
      1 cup milk
      6 oz Muenster cheese
      salt
      pepper
      parsley
      1 clove fresh garlic, minced

Preheat oven to 350°, then grease an 8-inch round pan (or a 9-inch square pan). Line the bottom of the pan with pepperoni slices (use approximately ⅓ of the total number of slices).

In a bowl, mix flour, egg, and milk. Break up cheese into small cubes and add to flour mixture. Stir in salt, pepper, parsley, and minced garlic. Then pour the mixture in pan and spread. Top with the remaining pepperoni.

Bake 30 to 35 minutes, till lightly brown. Cool for 20 minutes before serving.

Meat Lasagna *(From the Blue Box.)*

 1 lb lean ground beef
 ¾ cup chopped onion
 1 tbsp dried parsley
 2 tsp salt
 12 oz tomato paste
 2 cups water
 1 tsp sugar
 1 tsp garlic powder
 ½ tsp pepper
 ½ tsp oregano leaves
 8 oz lasagna noodles
 1 lb ricotta cheese
 8 oz shredded mozzarella cheese
 1 cup Parmesan cheese

In a large skillet, cook beef until brown. Add the chopped onions, parsley, salt, tomato paste, water, sugar, garlic powder, pepper, and oregano. Cover and let simmer, stirring occasionally. This will make the sauce. Meanwhile, cook the lasagna noodles and drain.

In an oblong pan, spread a little of the sauce, then add layers as follows: lasagna, sauce, cheese, and sauce; repeat until ingredients are used up, putting sauce on top. Cover with foil and bake at 350° for 30 minutes.

Barbecued Spareribs

 1 cup catsup
 2 tbsp Worcestershire sauce
 ⅓ cup wine vinegar
 1 onion, chopped (any size will do)

½ to 1 tsp pepper

Mix ingredients together and set aside. This recipe makes enough sauce for 2 or 3 lbs spareribs; simply double the ingredients if you need more.

Bake the ribs without sauce for 1 hour at 325°. Then add sauce on top and cook for 1 more hour. Serve with rice.

Oriental Tuna Casserole

10-oz can undiluted cream of mushroom soup
½ soup can of water
1 small onion, chopped
½ cup celery, chopped
pepper to taste
16-oz can white tuna in water, drained
⅓ cup roasted cashew halves
1½ cups crispy Chinese chow mein noodles

Mix soup and water; then add onions, celery, and pepper. Add remaining ingredients, including 1 cup noodles, and blend thoroughly. Finally, sprinkle top with the remaining ½ cup of noodles. Bake for 25 to 30 minutes at 325°, or until casserole turns bubbly. Serves 4.

Calzones

The "pouched pizza"

DOUGH

1 tbsp yeast
1 tbsp sugar
2 cups water
2 tbsp olive oil
6 cups flour
a dash of salt

Dissolve yeast and sugar in warm water, then add yeast, water, and olive oil to flour and salt. Mix together and knead dough for 5 minutes.

Cut dough into five equal-sized chunks and roll flat. Let the dough sit (and rise) while you prepare the toppings and sauce.

SAUCE — Basically, any tomato or pizza sauce will do. See the Good n' Easy Pizza sauce recipe below as an example. Serve the sauce warm, in a small dish on the side.

FILLINGS

> 1 lb mozzarella cheese
> ½ lb cheddar cheese
> 8 oz ricotta cheese (optional)
> sliced mushrooms
> vegetables
> pepperoni or other meats

As far as toppings are concerned, anything goes! Each person at the dinner table gets his or her own personal calzone, so meals can be made to order. First, coarsely grate the mozzarella and cheddar, then mix together ½ cup mozzarella, ¼ cup cheddar, and ¼ cup ricotta. Repeat this step until you have as much (or as little) as you want. All other ingredients are optional, and may be combined in any fashion.

For vegetarians, a spinach, mushroom, and broccoli calzone is delicious. Onions and green peppers also make good fillings. A few wild-and-crazy folks add chopped pineapple. For meat eaters, pepperoni, sausage, and hamburger are all fine choices. It helps to stir-fry the selected vegetables and meats in a pan before adding them to the calzone.

Place cheeses and fillings in the center of each pocket of dough. Fold in half and pinch the edges tightly shut so the ingredients will stay inside. Bake the calzones in a preheated 400° oven for 25 minutes, or until the dough turns light brown. Serve with a side dish of warm pizza sauce for dipping.

Good n' Easy Pizza

For dinner in a hurry. If you've just walked five weary miles through the cold rain on a mountain search-and-rescue operation, the last thing you want to do is spend a lot of time preparing a fancy dinner—you want some-

Pizza: The Fifth Food Group

Pizza changes from day to day on top of Mount Washington. What once started as a primitive combination of bread, sauce, and cheese soon evolved into a deluxe frying-pan pizza that took hours to prepare.

To feed a normal-sized crew, we used to make four large pizzas, cooked on silver cookie pans. Then one night, after a late evening search-and-rescue operation, the entire Lakes of the Clouds hut crew stayed unexpectedly at the Observatory for dinner. All those hungry, weary bodies wolfed down our precious pizza in just 15 minutes. To make a second, even bigger batch, we snuck upstairs and "liberated" two more trays from the State Park kitchen.

Senior Observer Norm Michaels remembers the origins of Rockpile pizza, during his first stint on the mountain in the 1970s. Back then, the pizza cook du jour was a burly man named Lee Vincent.

"Lee was the transmitter supervisor for WMTW-TV on the summit," says Michaels. "The transmitter building also contained the living quarters for the TV summit crew. It was adjacent to the old Observatory and was connected to it by a covered walkway.

"Cooking was one of Lee's hobbies, and we often ventured over there for dinner. Though the distance was short, the wind howled in the gap between the buildings, and the crossing was not always easy."

Today the pizza-making tradition continues. We still bring a few pies over to the TV building every now and then, even though the new Observatory stands on the far side of the summit, making the trip a rugged, rough, and unpleasant journey in bad weather. During a hurricane wind, rather than carry over a pizza by hand, we could probably just fling it off the tower and shout, "Catch!"

one else to spend a lot of time doing it! But just in case that doesn't happen, here's a pizza recipe that's easy to make.

DOUGH
>   1 package yeast
>   1 tsp sugar
>   1 cup warm water
>   1 tsp salt
>   2 tbsp olive oil
>   2½ cups flour

In a large bowl, dissolve yeast and sugar in warm water. Then slowly pour in the remaining dough ingredients and beat vigorously (about 20 strokes). Knead dough for 5 to 10 minutes. Cover bowl and let dough rise for about 5 minutes while you prepare the sauce.

SAUCE
>   ½ cup diced onion
>   8-oz can tomato sauce
>   ¼ tsp salt
>   ⅛ tsp garlic powder (or one clove fresh garlic, minced)
>   ⅛ tsp black pepper
>   hot red pepper to taste

Mix all sauce ingredients and stir. Then return to the dough. Grease hands with vegetable oil or olive oil and spread the dough on cookie sheets. Then spread the sauce over the top.

Preheat the oven to 425°.

TOPPINGS — Sprinkle Parmesan cheese and 2 tsp oregano on top of the sauce. Then add any other toppings, such as pepperoni or mushrooms. Finally, sprinkle the top of the pizza with 2 cups mozzarella cheese and pop it in the oven for 20 minutes. Makes 1 large pizza.

Gourmet Deep-Dish Pizza

Be warned: This dinner takes several hours to prepare (and you'll spend almost as much time cleaning up the dishes). But the results are worth it. This recipe makes 3 gourmet pizzas.

DOUGH

> 3½ cups white flour
> 1½ cups whole-wheat flour
> 1 tbsp Parmesan cheese
> 2 tsp salt
> 2 tsp sugar
> 1½ tbsp yeast (2 packages)
> 2 cups warm water
> 3 tbsp olive oil

In a large bowl, combine white flour, whole-wheat flour, Parmesan cheese, and salt. Mix together with a large fork. In a dish on the side, dissolve sugar and yeast in 1 cup warm water.

Next, add olive oil and dissolved yeast to flour mixture. Quickly pour in the extra 1 cup warm water and mix with a spoon until all particles are moistened. On a well-floured surface, knead dough for 10 to 15 minutes.

Pour a little olive oil (about 1 to 2 teaspoons) in the bottom of the original bowl, and replace the dough, turning so that all sides are coated with the oil. Then cover bowl and let dough rise in a warm place for 1 hour while you work on the sauce.

SAUCE

> 5 cloves garlic
> ⅓ cup diced onions
> ½ cup mushrooms
> 1 tbsp olive oil

First, flatten and slice garlic. Dice onions and slice mushrooms, then sauté with olive oil in a skillet for 5 minutes.

Meanwhile, in a medium-sized pot, combine the following ingredients:

> 29-oz can tomato sauce
> 12-oz can tomato paste
> 2 tbsp olive oil

2 tbsp hot red pepper
1 tbsp oregano
¼ cup cheddar cheese (shredded)
¼ cup mozzarella cheese (shredded)

Stir together all ingredients except cheeses. Place pot on burner and start to cook at medium heat, stirring occasionally. After 1 minute, add the sautéed garlic/onion/mushroom mixture and stir. Add the cheeses intermittently as you cook sauce on low heat for 45 minutes. That gives you time to prepare the toppings.

TOPPINGS

I cup grated Parmesan cheese
oregano
spinach
onions
sliced tomatoes
mushrooms
broccoli
olives
cheddar cheese
mozzarella cheese

Any combination will work, but be sure to use generous portions of onions and mushrooms. Chopped spinach works well, as do olive slices. Chopped broccoli heads also work, but the secret is putting them in the right place.

Now for the final step: assembling all the components. Take three large, cast-iron frying pans and grease the sides with olive oil. Yes, we use frying pans here on the Rockpile; this creates a deep-dish pizza pie.

Split up the dough and fold into shape in each frying pan. A fairly thin dough works best; it will thicken a bit in the oven. Be sure to run the dough right up the sides of the frying pan—this is a deep pizza. If you want, pour just a little more olive oil on the crust and roll it around so that it moistens the surface.

Once the dough is in place, sprinkle ¼ cup of Parmesan cheese on each one. Then add a dash of oregano. Only then pour on the warm sauce.

Spread with a spoon. Keep the sauce thick. Next, throw on toppings: spinach, onions, mushrooms, broccoli, and olives, in that order (omit one or more, to taste). Save the sliced tomatoes for later.

Finally, add shredded cheese. First, sprinkle on a thin layer of mozzarella, then a layer of cheddar, then more mozzarella. Place tomato slices on top, for decoration. Add a final dash of red pepper, oregano, or parsley flakes, to taste.

In an oven preheated to 375°, bake for 45 minutes, or until cheese starts to brown.

Vegetarian Meals

Pasta Primavera *(Contributed by Sarah Shor.)*

1 lb fettuccine or linguine
1 large head broccoli
2 tbsp olive oil
4 to 6 large cloves garlic, sliced
½ tsp salt
4 tomatoes, seeded and chopped
salt and pepper to taste
½ cup walnuts, lightly toasted
1 avocado, peeled and sliced into wedges

The first step is to boil a large pot of water. Add the pasta to the boiling water at about the same time you start to sauté.

Wash the broccoli, peel the stems, and cut them and the florets into bite-sized pieces. Then heat the olive oil in a heavy saucepan or a large skillet. Add the sliced garlic and stir-fry for 30 to 60 seconds over medium heat until caramelized. Be careful not to let the garlic get too brown. Add the broccoli and stir.

Next, toss in ½ tsp of salt and stir. Cover the pan and let cook at medium to medium-high heat for 5 to 7 minutes, or until the broccoli is just tender Add tomatoes and stir, letting them simmer until they are barely softened. Finally, add salt and pepper to taste.

Meanwhile, drain the pasta. For each serving, put pasta on a plate, cover with broccoli-tomato mixture, sprinkle walnuts on top, and add avocado wedges around the edge. Serves 3 to 4.

Simple No-Crust Spinach Quiche

A summit favorite.

16-oz package frozen spinach
8-oz package fresh mushrooms, sliced
1¼ cups extra-sharp cheddar cheese, cut in ½-inch cubes
16 oz cottage cheese

3 eggs
2 tbsp flour
black pepper
paprika

First, thaw and drain the spinach, and slice the mushrooms. Cut the cheese into cubes.

Place all ingredients in a large mixing bowl and blend with a wooden spoon. Then carefully pour the contents of the bowl into a large (9-by-13-inch) glass baking dish. Sprinkle the top with black pepper and paprika. Bake at 350° for 45 minutes to one hour.

Variations of spinach quiche can be made by substituting onions, broccoli, ham, or bacon.

Cheesy Broccoli Casserole

10-oz package frozen broccoli, slightly thawed.
1 cup (4 oz) extra-sharp cheddar cheese, grated
2 cups creamed cottage cheese
3 eggs
3 tbsp butter, cut in pieces
3 tbsp flour

Cut the broccoli into large chunks and place in a lightly buttered, 2-quart casserole. Set aside.

Grate the cheddar cheese, then add remaining ingredients to the cheese. Place in a food processor or blender, and purée. Pour over the broccoli and mix well.

Bake at 325° for about an hour. Check your cholesterol, and eat if you dare. Makes about 6 servings.

Kerosene Rice & Beans *(Contributed by Lynne Host.)*

Guaranteed to warm you on the coldest winter day. When pressed, the creator of this recipe acknowledges that "two or three tablespoons of black pepper is OK too." Adjust to your taste.

1 cup brown rice
5 or 6 cloves garlic, crushed
3 tbsp olive oil
4 onions, sliced
1 or 2 green peppers, sliced
28-oz can crushed tomatoes
1 can (14 oz) shelled beans

SPICES

19 tbsp black pepper (this is the "traditional" amount, but it can be adjusted to taste; the recommendation for "rookies" is 2 tbsp)
1 tbsp cayenne pepper
2 tbsp chili powder
paprika
crushed red pepper

Sawdust from the Logbook
November 1, 1995

Crew gives a booming rendition of "White Christmas," in honor of today's modest snowfall (2.7 inches). All we need now is a fireplace and some roasting chestnuts. Nuclear beans n' rice for dinner again tonight. No casualties this time.

Start by cooking 1 cup brown rice in 2½ cups of water to which you have added 2 tbsp of black pepper, one of the crushed garlic cloves, and about 1 tbsp of butter.

While the rice is simmering, heat 2 or 3 tbsp of olive oil in a large skillet and sauté the rest of the garlic (you'll know it's ready when it smells wonderful). Add sliced onions and green peppers, and continue to sauté.

While the onions and peppers are still crisp, add the spices (the amount of crushed red pepper is left to the cook's discretion). Sauté for 2 to 3 minutes, then add tomatoes and beans. Cook until bubbly, then reduce heat. Cook an additional 15 to 20 minutes. Add water if necessary.

Finally, add hot rice and serve (have plenty of tortilla chips, cold water, and sour cream available).

For an absolutely fiendish variation of this meal, known as Nuclear Rice & Beans, add ½ cup hot red pepper while sautéing the spices. Cook in a well-ventilated area.

Cabbage Noodle *(Contributed by Mark Ross-Parent.)*

An old Polish dish—and an early winter favorite on Mount Washington.

1 cabbage, medium size
½ cup cider vinegar
½ cup water
1 tsp salt
black pepper to taste
1 pound egg noodles
2 tbsp butter

Chop the cabbage into bite-size pieces and place into a large cast-iron skillet. Add vinegar, water, salt, and black pepper. Cover skillet and simmer for 1 hour, stirring occasionally. You may need to add water at times to prevent sticking.

Cook the egg noodles al dente, then drain them, add butter, and blend them with the cabbage. Cook an additional 5-10 minutes, and serve hot.

For an interesting variation, add one pound of cut-up Polish sausage to the cabbage while cooking.

Zucchini Pilaf *(Contributed by Lynne Host.)*

2 medium zucchini, diced
2 tbsp olive oil
2 cloves garlic, minced
2 tbsp butter
1 cup long-grain white rice
1½ cups chicken stock (or vegetable broth)
½ cup white wine
Parmesan cheese

Sauté zucchini in oil with garlic, then remove from the pan. Add butter to the pan and brown the rice. Put browned rice in a large saucepan, add chicken stock (or vegetable broth) and white wine, and bring to a boil (uncovered). Then place zucchini on top of rice. *Do not stir!* Cover and steam until rice is tender (approximately 20 minutes). Top with Parmesan cheese and serve.

Mushroom Stroganoff *(Contributed by Lynne Host.)*

    2 cups wide egg noodles
    2 tbsp olive oil
    1 lb fresh mushrooms
    3 medium onions, chopped
    3 cloves garlic, crushed and chopped
    1 tsp pepper
    1 tsp paprika
    2 tbsp parsley
    ½ cup white wine
    1 cup sour cream or yogurt

Cook the noodles and drain them. Meanwhile, in a large cast-iron skillet, pour in the olive oil and sauté the mushrooms, onions, garlic, and spices for 4 to 5 minutes (until just cooked). Add wine and cook for 10 minutes, stirring occasionally. Finally, add the cooked noodles and sour cream, and heat until warm.

Eggplant Parmesan *(Contributed by Helen Gerard.)*

I've heard people say that eggplants are proof of life in outer space, because obviously these strange-looking pods don't originate on Earth. But wherever in the universe eggplants come from, they sure are delicious. Contributed by a long-time Observatory volunteer, this favorite recipe demonstrates just how good eggplant can be.

    2 medium eggplants
    Italian bread crumbs
    6 eggs (or more), beaten
    spaghetti sauce (any flavor will do)
    Romano cheese
    Parmesan cheese
    mozzarella cheese, shredded

First, peel eggplants and slice into quarter-inch-thick slices. Dip each slice in a bowl of Italian bread crumbs, then into beaten eggs, then again into bread crumbs. (Start with a bowl of 6 beaten eggs for dipping; add more if necessary).

Spray cookie sheet with cooking oil. Place eggplant slices in single rows, then spray again with cooking oil. Bake at 325° until fork tender, approximately 45 minutes to an hour. (Rather than bake, another possibility is to fry the eggplant slices in hot oil until they turn a light golden brown. Just be sure to drain each slice between layers of plain white paper towels before going on to the next step.)

Now put a layer of spaghetti sauce in the bottom of a casserole dish. Next, add a layer of eggplant. Cover with another layer of sauce. Then sprinkle on Romano and/or Parmesan cheese. The amount of cheese can vary to taste.

Continue to alternate eggplant-sauce-cheese layers, ending with a layer of shredded mozzarella.

Bake uncovered at 325° for 30 minutes or until bubbly.

Green Rice *(From the Blue Box.)*

    10-oz pkg frozen chopped spinach
    2 eggs
    2 cups milk
    ¾ cup packaged, pre-cooked rice (or 1½ cups leftover regular rice)
    ⅓ cup onion, chopped
    1 cup shredded American cheese
    ½ tsp garlic salt

Cook frozen spinach. In a bowl, slightly beat the eggs and add milk. Add all remaining ingredients and stir. Pour into a 10-by-6-by-1½-inch baking dish. Bake at 325° for 40 minutes, or until firm. Makes 4 to 6 servings.

Desserts

When a blizzard swarms over Mount Washington, no one on the summit worries much about sugar or calories. (A glance at the ingredients in some of these desserts probably tells you that much.) The crew can always work off dessert by shoveling snow. In fact, dessert weighs people down so that howling, hurricane-force winds don't blow them away like leaves. (At least, that's a good excuse to use if you want to snatch the last piece of pumpkin pie.)

Eaten in moderation, these desserts are delicious.

Pumpkin Pie *(Contributed by Barbara Shor.)*

(With a secret ingredient)

3 eggs
¾ cup brown sugar
2 tbsp honey
1 tbsp maple syrup
½ tsp salt
1 to 2 tsp ginger
3 to 5 tsp cinnamon
½ to 1 tsp nutmeg
½ to 1 tsp allspice or cloves
2 cups cooked, mashed pumpkin
¼ cup half-and-half or cream
¼ cup bourbon
single crust for a 9-inch pie

In a large bowl, lightly beat the eggs with the brown sugar, honey, and maple syrup. Add the salt and spices. (If you like the flavor spicy and rich, as do most folks on the mountain, add a dash more of each spice. If not, go with a little less, to taste.)

Next, stir in the pumpkin and the cream. (Cream will make the custard heavier and richer than half & half.) Add bourbon. A good aged bourbon will make the pie smoother.

Pour the mixture into a 9-inch round pie shell (deep pie plates work best). Bake at 450° for 10 minutes, then reduce heat to 400° and bake for

45 to 60 minutes more. Start to test the pie at 40 minutes; when a knife poked in the middle comes out clean, the pie is done. Keep an eye on the crust—you may need to shield it to keep it from burning.

You might want to double this recipe, if you hope to have more than one slice at the dinner table—a single pie won't last long!

Peak Pineapple Pie

One day, summit volunteer Bonnie Logan noticed a large supply of unused pineapple pie filling in the Observatory kitchen. She corrected the situation by writing down this recipe.

> graham-cracker or vanilla-wafer crumbs for crust (about 1½ cups or 1 pkg, crushed)
> 1 can (21 oz) pineapple pie filling
> 1 pint sour cream (or 1 pint plain yogurt)
> 8 oz Cool Whip or other whipped topping
> 1 box (3.4 oz) vanilla pudding, prepared according to directions

In a medium-sized bowl, mix the pineapple filling with sour cream and half a container of topping. Then blend-in prepared vanilla pudding.

For the crust, simply line a 9-inch pie plate with crushed vanilla wafers or graham crackers. Fill the crust with the pineapple mixture, then place in the refrigerator to set. Before serving, spread the remaining half container of topping over the pie.

Yogurt Pie *(Contributed by Lynne Host.)*

When you only have 4 ingredients, you know you're in for an easy-to-fix dessert.

> 8-oz container whipped topping
> 8-oz container yogurt (any flavor)
> 1 graham-cracker crust
> fresh fruit (optional)

First, mix together topping and yogurt, and pour into a prepared graham cracker pie crust. Then put it in a freezer and chill for approximately 1 hour. Before eating, allow it to thaw for 5 to 10 minutes. Top with fresh fruit if desired. That's all there is to it!

> graham-cracker crust
> 1 package graham crackers
> ½ cup sugar
> ½ cup melted butter

Crush the crackers, then combine with sugar and melted butter. Mix well and press into a pie pan. Bake at 400° for 15 minutes.

Mile-High Calorie Pie *(Contributed by Mike Colclough.)*

Be warned: Simply reading the ingredients of this monster pie is enough to make you feel full. The real thing is a delicious, once-in-a-lifetime dessert.

> 1 stick of butter
> 1 cup flour
> 1 cup chopped nuts
> 1 eight-oz package of cream cheese
> 1 cup sugar
> 4 oz whipped topping, plus extra for topping
> 1 box instant vanilla pudding
> 1 box instant chocolate pudding
> 3 cups milk
> 2 to 3 thin chocolate bars, broken into large pieces
> 2 to 3 bananas

Cut the butter into the flour, blend in the chopped nuts, and press the mixture into a 9-by-13-inch pan. Bake at 350° for 15 minutes, then cool in the refrigerator.

Mix cream cheese, sugar, and whipped topping. When the "crust" is cooled, spread the cream cheese mixture on top.

Next, prepare the packages of instant vanilla and chocolate pudding, following the directions on the packages except use 1½ cups milk instead of 2 cups.

Spread the chocolate pudding in the crust and top with chocolate bars (or M&Ms, if you like). Then spread the vanilla pudding on top of that. Top with sliced bananas.

Finally, spread a little more whipped topping on top of pie. Refrigerate for at least 10 minutes, or until pie thickens. Serve chilled (and start an exercise program within three days of consumption).

Cocoa Mudslide Cake *(Contributed by Meredith Piotrow.)*

For best results, add icing just as you remove cake from oven. It takes a little timing.

> 1 cup butter or margarine
> 4 tbsp cocoa
> 1 cup water
> 2 cups white sugar
> 2 cups flour
> a pinch of salt
> ½ cup buttermilk
> 2 eggs
> 1 tsp cinnamon
> 1 tsp baking soda

ICING
> 1 cup white sugar
> ¼ cup butter
> 4 tbsp milk
> 1 cup chocolate chips

Preheat oven to 350°.

In saucepan, mix together butter, cocoa, and water, and bring to a boil. Meanwhile, in a separate bowl, mix sugar, flour, and salt. Add buttermilk, eggs, cinnamon, and baking soda, and mix well.

When the butter-cocoa mixture is at a boil, pour it over the other ingredients and mix together. Pour the batter into a greased cookie sheet or large cake pan and bake for 25 minutes or so.

Next, make the icing. Put the sugar, butter, and milk in a saucepan over medium-high heat. After it comes to a boil, remove from heat and quickly add chocolate chips. When the chips have melted, pour icing over warm cake.

Blueberry Streusel Cake *(Contributed by Sharon Jeffrey.)*

BATTER

> 3 cups flour
> 2 cups sugar
> 3½ tsp baking powder
> ½ tsp baking soda
> a dash of salt
> 2 cups sour cream (or yogurt)
> 4 eggs
> 2 cups blueberries

STREUSEL

> ¾ cup brown sugar
> 2 tbsp flour
> 3 tbsp butter
> 1 tsp cinnamon

ICING

> 2 tbsp milk
> 2 tbsp melted butter
> ½ cup confectioners' sugar (enough to make a loose icing)

To make the batter, sift together flour, sugar, baking powder, baking soda, and salt. Then mix in sour cream (or yogurt, if you prefer) and eggs; stir well. Next, grease a large (9-by-13-inch) pan and pour in the batter. Sprinkle blueberries on top.

The next step is to make the streusel. Cream together brown sugar, flour, butter, and cinnamon, then sprinkle on top of the batter (which is already in the pan). In a preheated oven, bake at 350° for half an hour.

Finally, to make the icing, mix milk, melted butter, and confectioners' sugar, and drizzle over the cake once it cools.

Oatmeal Cake *(Contributed by Meredith Piotrow.)*

> 1½ cups water
> 1 cup rolled oats
> ½ cup butter or margarine
> 1 cup brown sugar

1 cup white sugar
2 eggs
1 tsp vanilla
1½ cups flour
1 tsp cinnamon
1 tsp baking powder
1 tsp baking soda
a dash of salt

Preheat oven to 350°. Pour 1½ cups of boiling water over rolled oats. Let this mixture stand for 15 minutes.

Meanwhile, mix butter, brown and white sugars, eggs, and vanilla. Add the oatmeal mixture to the batter, and stir in the remaining dry ingredients: flour, cinnamon, baking powder, baking soda, and salt.

Bake in a greased and floured pan for 35 to 40 minutes. Then remove, allow to cool, and cover with icing. Which brings us to the next step:

BUTTER ICING

⅓ cup softened butter
3 cups powdered sugar
3 tbsp milk
1½ tsp vanilla

Blend or mix all ingredients until smooth, and add to the cake. To make orange icing, omit the vanilla and use orange juice instead of milk.

Apple Cake (Contributed by Lynne Host.)

2 cups whole-wheat flour
¼ cup oatmeal
2 tsp baking soda
1 tsp cinnamon
½ tsp nutmeg
4 cups tart cooking apples, diced
1 cup white sugar
1 cup brown sugar
½ cup oil
1 cup chopped walnuts
2 eggs, well beaten

1 tsp vanilla
confectioners' sugar

Mix together flour, oats, baking soda, cinnamon, and nutmeg, and set aside. In a large bowl, combine apples, sugars, oil, walnuts, eggs, and vanilla. Add to the flour mixture and stir gently with a wooden spoon.

Turn dough into a greased 13-by-9- inch baking pan. Bake in a pre-heated 350° oven for 50 minutes.

Finally, let the cake cool, and sprinkle it with confectioners' sugar. Cut into bars and serve.

Coffee Cake (From the Blue Box.)

TOPPING

    1 cup sugar
    2 tsp cinnamon
    ½ cup flour
    6 tbsp margarine, melted then cooled
    1½ tsp vanilla
    6 tbsp nuts

Mix together all ingredients, then set aside topping till later.

CAKE

    2 eggs
    1⅓ cups milk
    3 cups sifted flour
    1 cup sugar
    4 tsp baking powder
    1 tsp salt
    6 tsp margarine, melted then cooled

First, beat together the eggs and milk. Blend in sifted dry ingredients and margarine, being careful to mix only long enough to dampen all the flour. Pour into a greased 8-by-8-inch pan, then sprinkle with the topping. Bake at 350° for 35 minutes.

Pumpkin Cake

A quick dessert

4 eggs
1 cup olive oil
1 can (15 oz) pumpkin
2 cups sugar
2 cups flour
2 tsp baking powder
1 tsp baking soda
1 tbsp cinnamon
a pinch of salt

Place eggs, oil, pumpkin and 1½ cups sugar in a bowl. Beat together until smooth (use a large fork or an electric mixer).

In a separate bowl, stir together flour, baking powder, baking soda, cinnamon, salt, and the remaining ½ cup sugar. Slowly pour the flour mixture into the pumpkin mixture, stirring as you go. Blend thoroughly.

Very lightly grease a large glass baking pan (9 inches by 13 inches) with vegetable oil. Spread batter in the pan and smooth it with a spoon. It should be about ¾-inch thick. Finally, bake at 350° for 20 to 25 minutes. Allow to cool before serving; add frosting if desired.

Strawberry Meringue Torte *(From the Blue Box.)*

2 eggs
¼ cup margarine
1 cup sugar
1¾ cup sifted cake flour
2 tsp baking powder
a dash of salt
½ cup milk
¼ tsp vanilla
¼ tsp almond extract
1 quart fresh strawberries, crushed

Separate the egg yolks from the whites. Save the whites for the meringue. Use the yolks for the batter.

Combine butter and ½ cup of the sugar, and cream thoroughly. Add egg yolks one at a time, beating well after each addition. Then add the sifted dry ingredients, alternating with milk, vanilla, and almond extract. Stir continuously. Pour the mixture into two 8-inch, greased cake pans.

To make meringue, whip the egg whites with the other ½ cup sugar until very stiff, then spread over the remaining ingredients. Preheat oven to 350° and bake for 40 minutes.

Finally, allow the torte to cool, and spread strawberries on top. Add whipped topping if desired.

Butterscotch Brownies *(From the Blue Box.)*

> ¼ cup butter
> 1 cup brown sugar
> 1 egg
> 1 tsp vanilla
> ½ cup flour
> 1 tsp baking powder
> ½ tsp salt
> ¾ cup chopped nuts

Preheat oven to 350°.

In a bowl, beat the butter and sugar until creamy. Then beat in the egg and vanilla. In a separate bowl, sift the flour, baking powder, and salt. Finally, fold the flour into the sugar mixture and stir in the nuts.

Bake for 25 minutes in a 9-by-9-inch pan. Let cool before cutting into bars and serving.

Uncle Ferd Cookies *(Contributed by Barbara Shor.)*

If there was an actual Uncle Ferd, he had good taste. This is a wonderful thin, crisp sugar cookie. This recipe makes a large number of cookies, but they disappear fast!

> 1 lb butter
> 3 cups sugar
> 4 eggs

2 tsp vanilla (or almond extract)
7 cups flour

Cream the butter and sugar until fluffy. Then beat in the eggs, one at a time. Beat in vanilla. Slowly stir in the flour, one or two cups at a time. Work in the last two cups of flour with your hands, kneading slightly (Yes, you do actually need all that flour for proper crispness.) The dough should be buttery and should cling together in a mass.

Roll out the dough to a thickness of ½-inch on a lightly floured board. Cut into shapes with cookie cutters (If you put a little hole in the top of the cookies, they make excellent Christmas tree decorations).

Place cookies on greased cookie sheets, one inch apart. Be careful— they spread. Brush the tops of cookies lightly with beaten egg yolk, then decorate with sprinkles or colored sugars of your choice. (Don't use chocolate chips! They don't work.)

Bake at 350° for 5 to 10 minutes, until cookies are very lightly browned at the edges. If they cook too long, they get too hard. Remove from cookie sheet immediately.

Sticky Buns *(Contributed by Lynne Host.)*

2 packages yeast
½ cup sugar
¼ cup warm water
3 eggs
1 cup warm milk
5 cups flour
½ cup melted butter

Dissolve yeast and a little of the sugar in warm water and set aside to proof. Beat together eggs and rest of sugar. Add milk and 1 cup of flour, and continue to beat. Add yeast mixture and another cup of flour, and beat again. Finally, add melted butter and the remaining 3 cups of flour, and stir until mixed. Knead until smooth. Place the dough in a greased bowl, cover, and let rise for 2 hours.

While the dough is rising, start to prepare the "sticky" mixture:

4 tbsp melted butter
1 cup brown sugar
½ cup maple syrup
1 cup walnuts (chopped medium)

Mix ingredients together and spread across the bottoms of 2 greased baking pans (9 inches by 13 inches) to await the completed buns.

½ cup butter
sugar
cinnamon

Once the dough has risen, punch it down and divide it in half. Roll out to a thickness of ⅛-inch. Melt another ½ cup butter, and brush a thin layer over the dough. Then sprinkle with sugar and cinnamon. Roll up dough and cut rolls crosswise into 1-inch slices.

Now it's time to join the "sticky" component to the "buns." Place the rolled bun slices face down and close together in the pans, on top of the sticky mixture. Let them rise one additional hour. Then bake at 350° for 20 minutes.

Simply Delicious Spiced Hermits (Contributed by Norma C. King.)

1 cup raisins
1 tbsp orange juice
¾ cup shortening (not butter)
¾ cup granulated sugar
¾ cup brown sugar
2 large eggs, beaten
3 cups all-purpose flour
½ tsp salt
1 tsp baking soda
1 tsp ground cinnamon
1 tsp ground clove
1 tsp ground ginger
¼ cup molasses (dark or light)
2 tbsp water
¾ cup walnuts, chopped fine

Rinse raisins. Simmer in a shallow pan (small saucepan) over low heat with the orange juice only briefly (seconds instead of minutes). Turn off heat and let cool while working on the rest of the recipe. It will make the raisins plump up. Drain the raisins but reserve the liquid.

Cream together the shortening, sugars, and eggs (but save a small amount of beaten egg—about ¼ cup; you will need it later). Then sift the dry ingredients and add them to the butter-sugar-shortening mixture, along with the molasses and water. Finally, add the walnuts and plumped raisins. The batter should have a semi-thick consistency; add raisin liquid as needed.

Spread batter on a well-greased cookie sheet (with 1-inch sides). Brush top with the beaten eggs that you set aside earlier. Bake at 350° for 20 minutes, until cookies turn a light golden brown. Cut hermits into bars while hot, but let them cool in pan prior to serving. The results are chewy, moist, and delicious.

Doughnuts (Try all three varieties!) *(Contributed by Meredith Piotrow.)*

SWEET MILK DOUGHNUTS

> 1 egg
> 1 cup sugar
> 1 cup milk
> 5 tbsp melted butter
> 4 cups flour
> 4 tsp baking powder
> a pinch of salt
> 2 tsp cinnamon

SOUR CREAM DOUGHNUTS

> 2 eggs
> 1¼ cups sugar
> 1 cup sour cream
> 4 cups flour
> 1 tsp baking soda
> 2 tsp baking powder
> a pinch of salt
> 2 tsp cinnamon

BUTTERMILK DOUGHNUTS

> 1 egg
> ⅔ cup sugar
> 1 cup buttermilk (or use 1 cup plain yogurt)
> 2 tbsp melted butter
> 4 cups flour
> 2 tsp baking powder
> 1 tsp baking soda
> a pinch of salt
> 2 tsp cinnamon

Whichever flavor of doughnut you choose, the first step is to melt the butter. Then, mix all ingredients together to make a dough. Flatten dough to a thickness of one-half inch and cut into doughnut shapes.

Into a heavy pot, pour enough vegetable oil for the doughnuts to float in (5–6 inches) and preheat it to about 375°. Fry doughnuts until brown, then flip them over until the other side is done as well.

Sopaipillas (Contributed by Mark Ross-Parent.)

(Pronounced so-pa-*pee*-yas.) Instead of dusting the sopaipillas with powdered sugar, try serving them with fresh honey.

> 4¼ cups white flour
> 1¼ tsp salt
> 3 tsp baking powder
> 3 tbsp white sugar
> 2 tbsp shortening
> 1¼ cups milk
> vegetable oil (for frying)
> honey

The sopaipilla is the Mexican equivalent of a doughnut or fried dough. To begin, mix together the flour, salt, baking powder, and sugar. Cut in the shortening with a fork and a knife, or use a pastry knife. Add milk and stir with a fork until a soft dough forms.

Turn out the dough on a floured board and knead for 3 to 4 minutes. Then place the dough in a bowl, letting it sit for one hour.

Next, roll out the dough to a thickness of about ¼ inch and cut into diamond shapes. Pour 1½ inches of oil in a pan and heat to 375°F. Slowly add pieces of dough to the oil and turn occasionally to brown. Drain the cooked sopaipillas on paper towels and serve hot.

This recipe makes about 4 dozen. Serve with hot chili.

Rime Ice Cream *(Contributed by Ira Seskin.)*

This wintertime camping favorite, also known as "Rockpile Crunch," tastes best with a fresh crop of Mount Washington rime ice. If none is available, plain snow will do just fine. (Caution: In the good old days, all fresh snow was white and clean. Unfortunately, pollutants and acidity in the atmosphere now make it unwise to eat snow in many areas. If that's the case where you live, save this recipe for better days, when the air is clean again.)

    2 quarts rime ice
    14-oz can sweetened condensed milk
    chocolate chips
    M&M candies
    Reeses Pieces
    chopped nuts
    raisins

Place a 2-quart mixing bowl outdoors prior to a predicted snowfall (or fill it with existing rime ice). Carefully fold in the condensed milk until the mixture is slightly granular. If the milk is added too quickly, mix with a fork to correct the consistency. Fold in all remaining ingredients until it looks and tastes right. The mixture should be soft and creamy—like soft ice cream. Use ice pellets for an extra crunchy texture.

Appendix A
About the Mount Washington Observatory

The Mount Washington Observatory is a private, nonprofit organization funded by memberships and member donations, research contracts, and museum income. Since 1932 the Observatory has performed meteorological observations on the summit of New England's highest peak. In addition to hourly weather observations, the Observatory maintains and operates the Mount Washington Museum and supports educational programs about weather, science, and natural history.

Membership inquiries are welcome. Members receive a complimentary subscription to *Windswept* magazine, published four times a year. Other benefits of membership include free admission to the Mount Washington Museum, discounts in the museum gift shop, tours of the observatory, and eligibility for winter and summer EduTrips to the summit.

For more information, write or call:

The Mount Washington Observatory
2448 Main Street
P. O. Box 2310
North Conway NH 03860

Valley Resource Center: (603) 356-8345
Summit: (603) 466-3388
Internet: www.mountwashington.org

Appendix B

Conversions

English/Metric

1 mile = 1.61 kilometers   1 pound = 0.45 kilograms
1 foot = 30.48 centimeters   1 gallon = 3.8 liters
1 inch = 2.54 centimeters

Temperature

To convert Fahrenheit to Celsius, subtract 32, then multiply the result by five ninths (or 0.5555). Example: 50°F minus 32 = 18. Multiply 18 by 0.5555 = 10°C.

100°F = 38°C	−20°F = −28°C
80°F = 27°C	−40°F = −40°C
40°F = 4°C	−60°F = −51°C
32°F = 0°C	

Cooking Equivalents

(For those who want to convert recipes.)   500° F = 260° C
1 teaspoon (tsp) = 5 milliliters   450° F = 230° C
1 tablespoon (tbsp) = 15 milliliters   425° F = 220° C
1 ounce (oz) = 28 grams   400° F = 205° C
1/4 cup = 0.06 liters   375° F = 190° C
1/2 cup = 0.12 liters   350° F = 175° C
3/4 cup = 0.18 liters   325° F = 165° C
1 cup = 0.24 liters   300° F = 150° C
                                               275° F = 135° C

(Conversions are approximate.)

Appendix C

Books For Further Reading

Weather

Ludlum, Dr. David M. *The Audubon Society Field Guide to North American Weather*. New York: Alfred A. Knopf, Inc., 1991.

Watson, Benjamin A. T*he Old Farmer's Almanac Book of Weather and Natural Disasters*. New York: Random House, 1993

Williams, Jack. *USA Today: The Weather Book*. New York: Vintage Books, 1992.

I also heartily recommend the colorful magazine *Weatherwise,* published by Heldref Publications, 1319 18th Street N. W., Washington DC 20036.

Gretel Ehrlich's book, *A Match to the Heart* details the author's long road to recovery after being struck by lightning. The book also provides a powerfully beautiful description of the inner workings of a thunderstorm.

Geology

Raymo, Chet and Maureen E. Raymo. *Written in Stone*. Old Saybrook, Conn.: Globe Pequot Press, 1989.

Guidebook to Field Trips in Northern New Hampshire and Adjacent Regions of Maine and Vermont. New England Intercollegiate Geological Conference, 88th Annual Meeting. Edited by M.R. Van Baalen. Cambridge, Mass.: Harvard Printing and Publishing Services, 1966. (Very technical, very thorough.)

Van Diver, Bradford B. *Roadside Geology of Vermont and New Hampshire*. Missoula, Mont.: Mountain Press, 1987.

White Mountain History and Photography

Dobbs, David and Richard Ober. *The Northern Forest*. White River Junction, Vt.: Chelsea Green, 1995.

Nyiri, Alan. *The White Mountains of New Hampshire.* Camden, Maine: Down East Books, 1987. (Brilliant photography, neatly packaged. Now out of print.)

Putnam, William Lowell. *Joe Dodge.* Canaan, N. H.: Phoenix Publishing, 1986. (A thorough account of the life of the former Appalachian Mountain Club Huts Manager and founder of the Mount Washington Observatory.)

Recipe Index

General Index